CW00850696

Running Your Own
SMALL HOTEL

Running Your Own

SMALL HOTEL

Joy Lennick

Second Edition

Kogan Page
WORKING
for
YOURSELF
Series

Acknowledgements

The author thanks Mr and Mrs B David, Mr J P Miller of HM Customs and Excise VAT Office, Crown Buildings, Main Road, Romford, the staff at the Jobcentre, North Street, Romford, Mr Terry Fendt and Jeanne Spicer for their help.

First published in Great Britain in 1984
by Kogan Page Limited
120 Pentonville Road
London N1 9JN
Reprinted 1986
Second edition 1988
Reprinted with revisions 1989

British Library Cataloguing in Publication Data

Lennick, Joy
   Running your own small hotel—2nd ed.
   —(Kogan Page working for yourself series).
   1. Hotel management—Great Britain
   2. Small business—Great Britain—
   Management
   I. Title
   647′.94′068   TX911.3.M27

   ISBN 1-85091-540-7

Printed and bound in Great Britain by
Biddles Ltd, Guildford

Contents

refrigerator 65; General cooking utensils 66; Meat
slicer and food mixer 66; The automatic toaster 67;
Knives and chopping boards 67; The potato peeler 67;
Measuring scales 68; The kitchen water boiler 68;
Dish-washing machine 68; Cake tins 69; Extra storage
space 69; Hygiene 70; Disposal of rubbish 70

7. Daily Operation of the Hotel 71
An average day 71; Telephoned bookings 72; Postal
bookings 74; Printing needs 74; Settling customers'
bills 75; Pets 76; Laundry 76; Early morning tea 80;
The bar 80; The dining-room 83

8. Staffing 86
Engagement 86; Dismissal 87; Supervision 88;
Salaries 88; Legal requirements 89

9. Buying 90
Cash and carry outlets 90; Supermarkets 91; Door-to-
door delivery service 91; Freezer centres 91; Smaller
stores and shops 92; Shopping routine 92; Miscellaneous
93

10. Food and Drink 94
Familiar dishes are preferred 94; Set menus 96;
Ready-prepared food 98; Breakfast 99; Useful tips 99;
Drinks 105

11. Charging 107
Up-market hotels 107; Smaller hotels of similar
type 107; Low hotel-density areas 108; High hotel-
density areas 109; Your costs 110; Flexibility of
tariff 112

12. Getting Known 114
Advertising media 114; Advertisement content 115;
Special offers or events 116; Sources of business 117

13. Staying Ahead of the Competition 118
Encourage your guests to return 118; Competition from
larger hotels 121; Hotels with bars 122; Competing with
food or entertainment 123; Study the contents of

Introduction

Whichever side of the reception desk you are on, hotel life is fascinating and, for those concerned with catering, it can also be absorbing. However, hotel-keeping is also a way of life, and this should be taken into account before you take the irrevocable step. Its demands cannot be directly compared with those of any other business; the nearest example, perhaps, is the public house which serves meals, but here, of course, the doors are closed to the public for a period each day.

The novices who contemplate running a hotel would be well advised to allow for the fact that, while hotel life is very satisfying, it is also all-demanding. Working seven days a week for perhaps seven months of the year continuously can make you wonder if you've sold your very soul to the public, whereas in a shop, you have fixed opening and closing hours and a five-and-a-half- or possibly six-day week. There's a lot to be said for locking up at 5.30 or 6 pm, and having at least part of the weekend to yourself! Nevertheless, the shop-owner's criterion for job satisfaction is unlikely to be the same as the hotelier's, and vice versa.

Apart from being interesting, hotel work offers infinite variety. If you are to be head-cook and bottle-washer, the adage 'Variety is the spice of life' will fit like an oven-glove.

Most people appreciate it if you warm to them and care for their well-being (this, after all, should be the aim, especially in a small hotel where there is more personal contact between guest and proprietor). If you can achieve this naturally without overreaching yourself, all well and good; otherwise the public can consume and drain you before you know where you are and, however much you enjoy them and the work involved, mutual benefit will be derived by learning to hold back a little. Being over-involved when entertaining people can leave you feeling like a used tea-bag by the time midnight strikes. If you are the enthusiastic type, restraint is a difficult lesson to learn, but worth the effort.

Conversely, it would be unwise, unbusinesslike, and certainly not in your best interests, to act so detached as to deserve a 'cold fish' label. There are the odd, misplaced hotel proprietors who

9

would do well — and the public a good service — to find themselves an entirely different business to run, for it is doubtful whether such misfits achieve, or deserve, long-lasting success.

Before going a stage further into the hotel business, it is essential to examine your present standing in life, both in terms of financial and personal stability and security. Their importance should not be under-estimated. If they go hand in hand, think long and hard before changing your life-style. However, if you are reasonably secure financially, but feeling the urgent need of a stimulus or challenge which your present occupation denies you (assuming you like people and are socially adept), then hotel life may just be for you.

It is a fair assumption to make that many would-be hoteliers have, in the past, at least had a connection with catering in one form or another, and that running a hotel of their own has been a long-standing ambition. Anyone with experience and some catering expertise is obviously off to a flying start, but hotel life is so diverse, one needs to be both versatile and tough. Of course, the initiated are at an advantage, but the uninitiated need not lag behind if blessed with flair and common sense. One can be versed in the art of any cooking from pastry-making to elaborate French cuisine, or be only modestly endowed with culinary knowledge but able to shine as a general factotum.

You may be considering running a hotel for a variety of reasons. It could be that your present occupation is a dead-end, unfulfilling or totally boring. Perhaps you have been made redundant, inherited some money, or are just in the process of making a pipe-dream come true. If the latter — beware! It would be cynical to suggest that no dreams come true, but be prepared to shed, if not blood, a lot of sweat and a few tears. The lure of the country or coast, coupled with the desire to dazzle with your culinary skills, or play host/hostess, can be very tempting. The realities should be carefully considered. There are those who take on hotels misguided enough to believe that they can look forward to an 'eat, drink and be merry' sort of existence; they are in for a rude awakening! While there is no disputing that the atmosphere can be infectious and pleasing when all the various ingredients that go towards making a hotel successful gel, there is much hard work involved. However, there are hoteliers (especially those who double as barmen) who exude an air of bonhomie and always seem to be on cloud nine....

In days gone by when hoteliers generally had a slightly grand image, they were regarded as being well-heeled individuals who owned hotels. Of course 'grand' hotels do still exist, and it is likely that many of the owners are equally 'grand', but the purpose of this book is to cover smaller, more modest establishments whose owners are culled from all walks of life.

The 'poor' landlady — rich though she may have been — suffered the slings and torments of comedians' arrows. Even today, she is the butt of many a joke. Many landladies of modest guest houses are, quite legally, calling their establishments 'hotels', which is sometimes confusing to the public, and 'hoteliers' are rolling up their sleeves and performing any menial task they are obliged to. There are no clear demarcation lines.

The 'manager-hotelier' is a man to be envied. He is likely to have had training and experience and to pride himself on his expertise. It is also likely that he will have a more professional approach than the self-made hotelier. Usually, the manager-hotelier is to be found in an up-market hotel.

Sound mathematics are vitally important. Getting your sums wrong and landing yourself with an overdraft before your first guest arrives is obviously not a good way to start; a surprising number of people do just that. In this particular area, enthusiasm shouldn't be allowed to win over practicality.

Allow for all the obvious expenses if you are moving into a hotel, such as estate agents' fees, solicitors' fees and disbursements, stamp duty, and the cost of removal itself. After the move there are sometimes below-the-belt blows like the central heating breaking down (be vigilant) or someone accidentally smashing a washbasin. Of course, no one can foresee such events, but do cover such eventualities by insurance as soon as possible. Whatever business you run, there are bound to be such periodic difficulties.

A good start is linked with good timing. If, for instance, you consider buying a resort hotel at the end of the summer season, make quite sure you have adequate funds to see you through the leaner autumn/winter period. If your predecessor has obtained bookings for the quieter seasons, including Christmas and New Year, should you decide to open then, all well and good. It isn't always so. It might seem an impossible task to buy and run a flourishing hotel at the start, or in the middle, of the busy season, but at least you will be taking money right off. Being thrown in at the deep end does have its advantages!

Recessions apart, perhaps the climate is the biggest enemy of all. Oddly enough, good/bad weather doesn't always bode well/disaster. The blackest, wettest nights, especially in terms of short-stay guests, can have you on your toes more often than an unseasonably balmy evening, or the lead dancer in *Swan Lake*. The public, like fate, can be fickle and full of surprises.

'Ifs' are rife when running a modest 'do-it-yourself' hotel. If you can cope with someone losing their key and ringing the doorbell (slightly the worse for wear) at 3.00 am; if you can produce or rescue a crème caramel while answering the phone; segment a dozen-and-a-half grapefruits (between finding a stamp for Mrs B in room 2 and replacing a light bulb); ward off an ardent (business-wise) salesman while doing the accounts and calm down a dis-traught lady who has misplaced her engagement ring — more or less at the same time! — put your money down. It could be that you have found your vocation in life.

On the flip side of the coin, the perks of running a hotel can be many. Quite apart from personal satisfaction and fulfilment, and these surely count for much, you are — perhaps for the first time in your life — your own boss. Paradoxically, this gives an often false, but none the less enjoyable, sense of freedom. There are interest-ing people to meet, friends to be made, and a feeling — if you genuinely care for your fellow-man — that you have, in your own modest way, contributed towards making someone's holiday an enjoyable one. Just think, you and your hotel could be a nostalgic highlight for someone, somewhere, someday.

Now and then you will quite likely receive flowers, plants, choco-lates and money, unexpected little gifts, and invitations to visit other parts of the country or the world. All very welcome to be sure. You must at least have got something right! No less welcome are the touching 'thank you' cards and letters that will wing their way to you, and the heartening remarks in the guest book: 'Best *ever...*', 'Super hosts...', 'Delicious fare — will definitely be back!'. And, when guests (or their relatives and friends) do return, that's your bonus; you sowed your own seeds and reaped the harvest. So much cheaper and more satisfying than advertising.

Evaluate yourself

A sound exercise would be to list your traits — good and bad — your likes, dislikes, skills, family commitments and hobbies. It goes without saying that the person who doesn't suffer fools gladly (and some of the public are) is low on patience generally. One who is not in the least domesticated and can't boil an egg (even with staff, there always comes a day when one needs to) would be well advised to seek another business. Surely such people do not run hotels, you may say; you would be surprised. There's many a square peg in a round hole. Apart from invaluable assets like being able to cook well, and handling people individually and en masse, being versatile and flexible will stand you in good stead. And remember, patience and a good sense of humour will save *your* nerves. If you have a broad back, all well and good; if you have a broad mind too, all the better! Couples no longer feel the need to write 'Mr & Mrs Smith' in the register.

Examine your role in the life of the family and the importance to you of a social life, particularly if you contemplate a far-distant move. Once you are in the full swing of running a hotel, it will be a case of one-way traffic until the winter. Consider too, if you are moving children of any age, how the move will affect them: the loss of friends, school and familiar surroundings. It will be harder all round if they belong to the younger age group. Once it is accepted that you cannot be at their beck and call, they will doubtless benefit from the independence they will have to learn, but first-off, could very much resent sharing you. The eight-to-twelve-year olds may be an easier group for everyone concerned, but beware of disturbing teenagers! — they can be meaner than a bull on a cactus. Naturally, a lot depends on the personality and attitude of each individual, whether adult or child. There are plenty of distractions for children (too many as regards homework) particularly if your hotel has a games room or play area and there are children staying as guests. There will be occasional invitations in the evenings, during weekends and at holiday times, to join in visiting families' activities, and another perk for children is the opportunity for earning the odd tip or two.

Another very important factor in respect of children of any age is to satisfy yourself that schools are adequate and, particularly with regard to the older age group, what employment prospects there are in the area. The latter factor is worrying in view of the economic climate and depends largely on the child's chosen field and adaptability. If a child is interested in catering and attends a course to further his ambitions, the advantages are obvious.

There are those who take to hotel life like fish to water and thrive on almost total involvement, and others who find they are resentful of the intrusion into their private lives.

Depending on how close-knit a family you belong to, consider the pros and cons of moving away from them. What seems at first like a welcome breathing space can later become a void — especially if there are sick or aged parents and relatives involved. Personal circumstances are so diverse, it is impossible to generalise or give specific advice, but do discuss all aspects of such a venture with your nearest and dearest, and satisfy yourself as to their welfare in your absence, especially when moving far from home. Once the season starts, assuming you belong to the 'short pocket brigade', it is very difficult to get away from the hotel.

Consider, too, the effects of being tied in relation to hobbies. If you are heavily involved in the running of even quite a small concern, in the busy season there won't be an abundance of time left for golf, tennis or whatever. It does, naturally, depend on how much you give of yourself (or *have* to give) to your guests and business; how efficient and organised you are; your own family demands, and the state of your bookings. The load eases in winter, discounting the Christmas and perhaps New Year periods and depending on whether you choose to open or not. If you are happy with sedentary hobbies, life can be relatively easier — between re-decorating, refurbishing and renovating that is. That said, it is still possible, with good organisation and a little assistance, to pursue hobbies in the quieter seasons.

The personal involvement

As in other aspects of running a hotel, your involvement hinges on many things. Beginning at the guest house/small hotel end of the scale, it is quite likely that you may run your business with just one, maybe two assistants, possibly your wife/husband/relative/ friend. Many small hotels are run as family concerns. Once you have listed your various duties, you will be able to establish a routine both desirable and workable for your particular business. For a fluid working pattern, duties have to be dovetailed. If, for instance, your husband or whoever is an excellent cook/driver/ shopper, and handy with a hammer to boot, and you are happy performing various chores, well and good. Add waiting on tables, arranging flowers, attending to guests' needs, keeping accounts and an eye on bookings, typing letters and tariffs etc, and you will realise the need for flexibility and versatility. To make it all come together and really work well, your heart must be in it.

If, from the point of view of a guest — say a young mum — it's raining outside, the baby's teething, the dinner wasn't quite up to the usual standard *and* she's confronted with your gloomy countenance, it could put the final damper on that particular lady's holiday. A smile costs nothing. So your feet and back ache, and your other half's in a mood? That's not the guest's problem. Don't wear your heart on your sleeve. When in the public eye, you must give them the image they want. After all, they're footing the bill!

Up the scale, in terms of hotel size, if you are a part-owner/ manager, here again the same principles apply but, because of necessary delegation of work and involvement with staff, you need extra tact and a well-honed ability to organise. In this situation, the experienced person will usually score. Nevertheless, your involvement — regardless of the size of the hotel — will depend on so many imponderables, mainly tied up with your financial standing and personal requirements.

Moving into a larger hotel

If you take to hotel life — and it can be very addictive — it is possible that you may decide, after a couple of years in your small establishment, to consider running a slightly larger one. Although many basic principles apply in the running of hotels, regardless of size, it stands to reason that the larger the hotel, the more staff required to run it. If, for instance, you feel competent and able to run a 10-bedroomed hotel with just one full-time and one part-time assistant (and many do) it could well work, when planning the running of a 15-to-20-bedroomed hotel, simply to double your staff, although you may find it viable and more convenient to alter the balance, ie, still to employ one full-time person, but to treble your part-time assistants. There is an abundance of likely sources from which to choose staff, from agencies and Jobcentres to English-language schools and a variety of colleges — more especially in the height of the season — just when part-time staff are most needed. To cull staff from a catering college in particular makes good sense all round. Provided they are not just employed as washer-uppers, working in a small hotel is an excellent training ground for youngsters with ambition.

You need have no qualms about the employee/employer relationship; if you are sensible, it should work to mutual advantage. Be firm but fair, make working hours and various duties crystal clear, and pay a reasonable wage. Remember, a good, reliable and honest worker is worth far more than his wages. Luck plays a large part here. Occasional illness and other unforeseen circumstances are bound to cause hiccups, hence your need to fill various roles.

Chances of success

Quite apart from the obvious hard work and application required, there are no hard and fast rules to follow for success of any kind, and there is no easy path. Learning by one's mistakes seems to be commonplace. Diligent groundwork is vital, and your ultimate success or otherwise can (coupled with other considerations) be dependent on its soundness. Do your homework thoroughly. Satisfy yourself as to audited accounts, position — and state — of hotel and future bookings. These are crucial points to check out before committing yourself. Have all the necessary information in black and white; there is no room for gullibility. Occasional problems are bound to arise in any given situation but, given a keen desire to succeed and applying that desire in a practical way, and given health, stamina and a stubborn will, it is surprising what you can achieve.

Obviously, financial gain, quite apart from a high level of personal satisfaction, is both desirable and necessary, for to see one's capital outlay grow is surely the ultimate aim. This is sometimes easier said than done! Be warned that, if your capital is too modest — unless unusual circumstances intrude — you will have to wait for several years before showing a true profit. Borrowing too much is a common trap and, having started off on the wrong foot, it can take a long time to emerge victorious, and all the sound advice, text-book information and help available will fall on stony ground if you are over-ambitious.

You will, of course, need to take out a personal wage but, if your capital outlay cuts your finances to the bone, it will have to be a modest one. However clever you are with figures, it is impossible to balance high outgoings with low incomings, let alone show a profit. That said, providing you are sensible and your hotel — large or small — is clean, welcoming and comfortable, and offers a better than average menu (always strive to improve) and you, as host or hostess, do your best, you could be one of the lucky, deserving — deserving being the operative word—hoteliers in the business.

Chapter 1
What Type of Hotel?

Having made the decision to go into the hotel business, the next step is to decide what type of hotel you would like to run.

Converting your home into a guest house or hotel

Larger than average private houses can be converted into guest houses or hotels with surprisingly good results and, with careful planning, can pay off. Position here is all-important; a house situated away from main roads, surrounded by a maze of suburban houses, is not a good proposition. In the right spot, the venture is well worth considering, especially if you own your property outright or have only a small mortgage outstanding. Remember, though, that you are starting off 'cold' and make allowance for the fact. You may be an expert cook and gracious host but the public at large (however clever your advertising) are ignorant of the fact until they actually pass through your portals. After a probationary period, of course, your bookings could soar, but it all takes time.

In the first instance, you will need to know of any planning restrictions, special requirements and details of registering as a guest house or hotel. Also check (as you would if buying another property) that no new roads, car parks, or buildings of any kind which could adversely affect your business are planned for your immediate area.

Confirm also that there are no restrictions in the deeds of the house which would affect its use as a guest house or hotel. There may be more red tape to cut through if your house — even in its present state — is to be the only guest house or hotel in the road. Neighbours may object to the possibility of increased noise, perhaps smells, or the persistent use of adjacent parking spots and the to-ing and fro-ing of cars where a forecourt or parking area is provided. For your peace of mind, quite apart from any legal aspect, consult your solicitor as to any restrictions which may be imposed. In the case of actual building work being necessary (especially when converting attics and so on) detailed plans must be submitted to your local council and planning permission applied for. Should your application be successful, it is then likely that a higher, commercial, rateable value will be placed on your property.

Consult your solicitor, accountant and bank manager to discuss the whole matter and to examine your financial position. If they give you the go-ahead, and there is work to be carried out, immediately obtain several quotes from builders and decorators. The process can be of long or short duration, depending on the amount of work demanded by the existing layout of your house and the facilities already available. In the main, you will need to have a hot and cold water basin in each bedroom, and the single bedrooms should not be smaller than 60 square feet. Also, a reliable central-heating system is essential. Apart from a residents' lounge and dining-room, and the usual furnishings, ensure that there are sufficient showers, bathrooms and toilets. The standards, and any extra comforts, would naturally be dictated by funds available.

Budget carefully; providing bedding, linen, crockery and kitchen equipment, etc, not to mention furniture, can be a costly business. Scour advertising papers and second-hand shops, genuine bankruptcy and house/hotel contents sales; all are valuable hunting grounds.

Keep some reasonable accommodation for yourself and your family. It is surprising what some proprietors will endure, from sleeping in the basement (behind the kitchen) with no natural light or windows, to squeezing into a box-like room with no space to swing a string of sausages. Unless you are very Bohemian, just one season living in such cramped conditions will surely wear you down.

Apart from the actual cost of building or structural alterations and decorating, also allow for some fire-work. Fire precautions are necessary where a guest house or hotel sleeps more than six people, so if you plan running such an establishment, a fire certificate will be essential. Anyone ignoring this ruling is acting illegally. Even where basic fire prevention work is carried out in anticipation, it will need to be inspected and, if necessary, brought into line with the Fire Precautions Act of 1971.

Your house may require only minimal fireproofing or, depending on the size and type of building involved, quite a lot. Each year, the requirements become stricter, and rightly so. Do not let this deter you, for they do vary, and a reasonable amount of time is given for the work to be carried out. Fire doors are required, and partition walls of insufficient strength may need reinforcement to meet certain standards; some electrical work is also involved. Quotes should be obtained from several firms and compared. Once installed, it is standard practice for fire-work to be checked periodically. Twice-yearly tests are usually adequate. Get in touch with your local Fire Chief, who will put you on the right path.

It is worth considering taking in a permanent resident or two, but do tread warily here. It is a sad fact that some of the more elderly residents — appreciative guests though many are — are too proud and independent to face up to the fact that they can no longer look after themselves. Confirm that any older would-be residents are in good health, for it is kinder in the long run to discuss their future should ill-health occur. Apart from people of independent means, there are always students to consider, and this possibility is discussed in a later chapter.

Bed and breakfast only
After some deliberation, you may decide that you would prefer to start off with a bed and breakfast only guest house or hotel. Apart from having commercial appeal, bed and breakfast establishments also attract visitors on long journeys as a stopping point, plus tourists — both native and foreign — and quite a number of holiday-makers who prefer to eat their main meals in a variety of restaurants. Run capably, such a business would give you ample time for hobbies, to look after your family, or work part time in another field. This arrangement could be quite satisfying and less time-consuming, especially as one is not as tied as when running a bed, breakfast and evening meal concern. The income may prove to be only modest, depending, naturally, on how many rooms you let and your overheads, but if your position and reputation are good, you could do brisk business in the summer season and, indeed, throughout the year, should you wish to. As bed and breakfast proprietors often have another string to their bow, bringing in a second income, and the profit margin on bed and breakfast is quite good, they sometimes stand to do better than the small guest house or hotel proprietors offering bed, breakfast and evening meal.

Despite the vast number of people who now prefer a 'healthier' breakfast of fruit juice, muesli and fruit, and brown bread and honey (which, if wise, you will stock anyway) the fried breakfast is still popular with the majority. Go easy on the oil or fat (non-stick frying pans need very little of either). Compared with a three-course meal, it would seem simplicity itself to cook bacon, eggs, fried bread and sausage, accompanied by perhaps mushrooms or tomatoes. Unfortunately, there are some instances — thankfully only a few — where the fried bread is either like cardboard or a soggy mess, the egg dried and rubbery or — worse — cold! The bacon either under- or over-cooked, and the tomatoes or mushrooms 'done' to death.

The 'bed and breakfast only' proprietors should afford the time and effort to enable them to claim honestly, 'The best breakfast for miles!' and advertise the fact. Ensure that fruit juice is chilled, varied and pure; offer a variety of cereals — including porridge — instead of the same, boring old cornflakes. As to the main course, do vary it. For many, kippers and haddock make a welcome change from the eternal fried breakfast. Keep portions as generous as you can possibly afford — there's no future in plonking a cocktail sausage, half a rasher, and a quarter of a slice of fried bread on the table. If you complete the meal with reasonably hot (or at least warm) toast and the offer of more tea or coffee, it will be well worth the extra effort.

You may, however, be more ambitious, and decide to start off in the hotel business by buying your own establishment. The choices lie between holiday and commercial hotels.

Seaside family hotel

Should you go for a small, family-type hotel, the location is all-important. If the hotel is at the seaside, try to ensure that it is within reasonable walking distance of the beach; not everyone travels by car. A surprising number of holiday-makers still arrive by train and coach. Specific hotels are chosen because of the facilities offered, not least the proximity of the sea. Senior citizens and younger children (not to mention harassed mums and dads) appreciate this. Of course, generally speaking, the nearer the sea, the dearer the hotel... However, should you tuck yourself too far away from the beaten track, your business could suffer; look for something in between. While it may seem to be stating the obvious, enthusiasm can outweigh good sense, and once purchased, 'white elephant' hotels are not easy to dispose of.

Families with younger children usually look for a baby-sitting service. This is, more often than not, less daunting than it sounds. Large doses of sun, sea and air combine to ensure that the little darlings usually sleep soundly. (In a family hotel, an intercom/listening-in system is most useful.) Some hotels prefer taking children over the age of five, for babies mean bottles etc and bed-wetting (not only the prerogative of the tiny tots either) can be a bind. Provide rubber sheets for younger children, just in case; it is upsetting and embarrassing for parents, as well as hotel keepers, to find that new mattresses have been spoiled. Bored youngsters can be a handful, but not all the little ones spend their time filling up loos with toilet rolls and flicking cereal at mater. Keep a small supply of books and toys for their amusement; it is pleasing to all to have happy, contented children staying. Having recovered from the journey itself and acclimatised themselves to their new surroundings, children are remarkably resilient, often more than they are given credit for. The troublesome ones (except in the case of genuine illness) are mostly the product of stupid parents, who continually stuff their offspring with candy-floss, ice cream and chips, interrupt established routine to suit their own purposes, and give in to their every whim. Should you have the misfortune to house such a family, suggest they breakfast or dine a little earlier than the other guests — it will be worth the bother. Fortunately, such families are in the minority.

On the plus side, planning children's menus can be fun and a test of your ingenuity; it is reward enough when youngsters' eyes widen like saucers at the sight of a colourful creation and they follow up with a heartfelt 'Ooo!'.

Each individual must make his own decision on which age limits to accept. Take in too many babies and small children and your hotel could soon resemble a crèche — thus putting off some childless couples, single people and some of the older generation. On the other hand, should you consistently book in a much higher proportion of elderly people than young or middle-aged guests, then your establishment could, all too easily and quickly, take on a sort of 'rest home' atmosphere. There is no disrespect intended here; all age groups are due the same consideration. For a workable, happy mix, an excess of one age group should be avoided if possible. A 'family hotel' should be construed as meaning just that — the whole family, from grandchild to grandparent, with various ages between. Of course, the balance will be tipped from time to time. If you should have a preference for a particular age group, your needs can be catered for by the careful wording of advertisements, although from a business point of view, you will find that specific groups are best catered for in the quieter seasons. At both ends of the age scale, the demands are slightly different but the needs are often the same.

During bank holidays and school summer holidays, it is natural to expect a higher ratio of children than senior citizens and, inevitably, vice versa in the spring, autumn and winter. The sheer variety of ages and people is part of the charm of hotel life. Once you become acclimatised to catering for different age groups, you will be able to set the scene accordingly.

Having decided upon a family hotel, you then have to consider what facilities to offer. A games room or, at the very least, a play area, counts a lot for all-round enjoyment, especially when the weather takes a nose-dive. A modest snooker or table-tennis table is worth its weight in gold on a wet evening, if you have the room. Popular too are card tables and various games — including, on occasion, bingo. This will depend on the crowd you have in — remember, it's a bundle of fun for some and a big snooze for others. For all those who like being organised, there will be many who prefer to do their own thing. See that there is a plentiful and varied supply of reading material in the residents' lounge and guests' bedrooms; this is appreciated. Subtle and varied background music during mealtimes (masking the scraping of cutlery and an occasional noisy infant) and in the evenings also adds to a more relaxed atmosphere. And, whether your hotel has large grounds or a modest garden, take full advantage of either; a pleasing garden and umbrellaed tables also attract passing trade. More than ever before, particularly in the quieter seasons, people take a chance and shop around for suitable accommodation. If your position and 'shop window' are sufficiently attractive, they pay off tenfold. People *do* ring the bell because: 'Your curtains look so crisp, I just knew your hotel would be clean . . . ', or 'Your bar and dining-room look so inviting, I do hope you have a vacancy . . . '.

People in general today, having travelled more widely, demand — and why shouldn't they? — better sanitation and washing facilities. The days of the single, chain-pull, toilet and one bath (with the plug thrown in twice a week) hotel are rightly numbered. Wherever possible, showers en suite are the perfect answer with, of course, sufficient separate loos and a bathroom or two (depending on hotel size). Stories of seedy rooms, broken wash-basins and damp linen still circulate but are, thankfully, on the decrease. More and more people expect — and deserve — value for their money.

A superior seaside hotel

Should your penchant be for a more exclusive hotel, catering for sophisticated palates can be rewarding, particularly if you and your staff — and here you will need staff — aim at a high standard of cuisine. The main drawback is money, or rather lack of it. The hotel offering a more exciting table must also provide plushier sur-roundings to complement the catering.

If you contemplate buying a run-down, but potentially promis-ing, establishment, do be careful about its position. Obviously, you would have to pay more for scenic or sea views, but could set your tariff accordingly. Should you choose a property — however fetching — tucked in among family guest houses making modest charges, it would not have the same appeal for the sophisticated holiday-maker, and your higher tariff would stick out like a sore thumb. Often, the more discriminating guest will request, not only a shower en suite, but a bathroom. If these facilities are already installed in the hotel of your choice, that's fine; if they are not, carefully consider the cost of installation.

You have to speculate to accumulate — that is common know-ledge — and, in the long run, it will probably pay off to do so but, in the meantime, do ensure that you have a sufficient cash flow from your own or the bank's coffers. Vast numbers of business people have large overdrafts; it is a way of life for many and, if you come from a self-employed business background, you will probably be familiar with this situation. On the other hand, if this is your first business venture and you have been used to a regular and fixed wage — and budgeting accordingly — you will need to adjust your ideas. Until you are firmly established, and even then the balance can tip either way, your income is bound to fluctuate, the main cause of the largest fluctuation being the season itself. Plan well ahead; with the summer trade in full swing and the money flowing in nicely, you can be lulled into a false sense of security. Don't wait until the autumn to advertise winter breaks. Too many practise false economies and live to regret it. 'Advertising costs money!' some say, 'We'll just see how things go...'. Don't let the grass grow under *your* feet.

If you are not already familiar with the more specialised demands of running an up-market hotel, it would certainly be advisable, if not imperative, for anyone considering such a venture to take a catering or business management course, or at least brush up on the subjects.

A country location

If you decide on the country rather than a seaside location for your hotel, of whatever type, comb your chosen county well. Positioned near a river or lake, in a spot of outstanding beauty — near a castle, famous building or pretty village, your hotel is at an obvious advantage. Do bear in mind, though, that all such places are seasonal. Plumping for a 'character hotel' in a near-inaccessible wood, miles from anywhere, is not a good idea, generally speaking, but even here there are exceptions for, if the hotel has an interesting history, is outstandingly beautiful, and serves food fit for the angels, the news will eventually get around. Wherever you are situated, if facilities are too far-flung or meagre, consider the vagaries of our English climate! For some, the desirability of being near a farm or riding stables is considerable. Converted barns, oast houses, water-mills, stables, etc, all have a special charm of their own, although established businesses housed in such appealing places will fetch a handsome price. Be sure, too, that *you* will enjoy living in a remote area.

Development area

Situations do occasionally arise where rumour has it (you may even know a property developer) that a particular area, for whatever reason, is 'ripe for a boom'. Perhaps a new airport is on the drawing board, or a shopping precinct coupled with a bank or insurance building is due to be erected. Where a hotel is on the market near such a place, waste no time in making enquiries (should you prefer to live in a town) and, if you actually decide on one with any new development completed and due to open, contact the people in the new concerns. Airports, banks, and commercial organisations have a constant stream of visitors from all over the country and abroad. You could be on to something big.

Impulse buy

In a situation where you can bide your time a little, there is nothing to lose and perhaps much to be gained by exploring all business opportunities. Make tentative enquiries, visit the area involved. Have a good look round and ask questions. Even if the outcome is disappointing, it is better than jumping feet first into buying the second hotel you see in an area which leaves much to be desired. Of course, should it so happen that a run-down area suddenly blooms, time is definitely of the essence. Inflated rents and rates and property prices have to be watched here. Luck plays a large part; it can be a case of being in the right place at the right time. If you do give in to a whim and buy an eye-catching hotel in a desirable part of a town, it is easy, if slapdash, to miss, or hardly notice in your excitement, all those streets round about with peeling paintwork and a generally run-down look. It really is essential that you explore trade possibilities and expectations, and take in the general appeal of the area in which you would like to set up business, before committing yourself.

An easy mistake to make when buying a hotel is to choose a location that is a personal favourite, letting the heart rule the head. However fine the sand and lovely the scenery, do sound homework before signing on the dotted line. If you really must move to a pretty village, the tourist board may be able to furnish you with figures showing just how many people are likely to head your way. Business in such places could be humming in summer and dwindle to a trickle once the summer sun goes down. It pays to study a map and get in touch with the local tourist boards in many areas before making up your mind.

If you have set your sights on a larger, more popular resort, you could hardly do better than choose a large seaside resort where business is brisk, such as Blackpool or Bournemouth. The Blackpool illuminations are famous and lure holiday-makers from far and wide.

Around 1.5 million visitors a year stay in Bournemouth and, although figures fluctuate, it continues to be a very popular resort. There is, and obviously needs to be, a high density of hotels of all sizes, and competition is, therefore, keen between hoteliers. It is a centre for students of English, and apart from being an excellent base for trips into the lovely Dorset countryside and the New Forest, Bournemouth is notably clean. Sadly, this cannot be said for all of our once popular seaside resorts. Much care and money is lavished on the parks, walks, verges etc, the beaches are good and plentiful, and shopping and other facilities excellent. Another strong point in Bournemouth's favour is its ability to entertain whatever the time of year; there are always pantomimes at Christmas, at least one good play or comedy running all-year round; several cinemas showing up-to-date films, and numerous wine bars, pubs and restaurants, a couple of casinos, several clubs, a skating rink and an orchestra. Knowing that the influx of visitors doesn't cease as soon as the sun sets on September can be a great comfort.

A larger hotel

Should you aspire to running a larger hotel, again, you have to decide whether you would prefer to attract a middle-class clientele of, say, families and general passing trade, or cater for the more wealthy. There is quite a difference (or should be) between menus and tariffs, facilities and service available. Your plans can be as elaborate or as simple as your pocket and taste allow. Either way, the more value for money you can give the better. Remember, the hotel trade in general is very competitive, and you have numerous unseen competitors to contend with — abroad in particular — offering fantastic money-saving package deals. You can opt for a 'sing-along, bingo evenings and chicken-in-the-basket' type atmosphere, or a quieter — resident musician — set-up, where the accent is on less frantic entertainment and the cuisine comes highly recommended. Of course, there are many in-betweens. It is very difficult to cater for everyone's tastes under one roof. A large, bustling family hotel, however clean and welcoming and however wholesome the cooking, does not have the same appeal to the couple looking for more restful surroundings, avocado vinaigrette and steak Diane, plus an intimate dance-floor. Food should provide the key you are looking for. Good, honest home-cooking without frills will go down a treat in a family hotel but a cordon bleu cook would do well to consider — whatever the size — a more exclusive establishment, or a hotel that is less family-orientated.

Commercial guest houses and hotels

A commercial guest house or hotel may hold a particular appeal for you. Apart from other obvious considerations, it is probable that the most successful are easily accessible, and either in or near to a town. The commercial traveller will usually need to be near a major road or have easy access to one. A comfortable television lounge and bar are welcomed, as are drinks machines in the foyer or facilities in bedrooms, and televisions or radios and telephones in the guests' bedrooms, along with, if at all possible, a desk or writing table.

The main difference between the usual holiday-maker or weekender and the travelling salesman is the need for more flexible mealtimes and the availability of snacks. Because of drawn-out appointments and late-running meetings, their comings and goings are often erratic. At one end of the scale, you can offer a flexible, efficient service in comfortable surroundings for the salesman with a modest accommodation allowance and, at conference level, or for the executive, you can offer the same efficiency and flexibility, with extras, in a plushier setting. It all depends on your aims and your resources. However, the commercial traveller is just as likely to head for a family hotel, for the tariff is often more sympathetic to his pocket. Regular travelling salesmen are a welcome and good source for 'bread and butter' trade, so treat them kindly.

Parking

A crucial point to consider — wherever you are situated — is parking space, even if it means giving up a portion of garden or forecourt. Hanging baskets, awnings, flowering and shrub-tubs can all combine to recompense for garden lost and, during the evening, lighting effects can create wonders. Everyone knows of the frustration those ubiquitous yellow lines breed and an existing car park is a blessing. Look out for hotels with little or no parking space available, and check that there are sufficient parking facilities close by. Many enthusiastic motoring guests put much store by the safe-keeping of their vehicles.

Chapter 2
Starting Up

Having decided to go into the hotel business, and agreed upon the
type of hotel, the next consideration is the premises, if you plan to
buy into the business.

Leasehold or freehold property

While there is no doubt that freehold property is more popular and
desirable, many promising hotels are leasehold. They can be an
excellent proving ground for the newcomer, but it is well to proceed with caution. Short leases of three to seven years are common
in business, but the shortest usually apply more to shops and other
premises rather than to hotels. In general, the longer the lease the
better; for example, if you took a new 15-year lease on a hotel, and
decided to move up the ladder after only three years, the remaining
12 years of the lease would be quite adequate for another
purchaser (and his bank) to consider favourably. No lending bodies
would entertain loans where the borrower's capital is small, and
the lease very short. A loan of, say, £50,000 towards the purchase
of a leasehold hotel costing £90,000 with only a four-year lease left
to run, would be a wild gamble.

Larger leasehold hotels can be bought for the same price as
small, freehold ones, so would offer a newcomer a better chance of a
higher return on his money if the rent were reasonable and he had
done his homework properly. A 15-bedroom hotel has greater
potential than one with eight bedrooms, but the owner has to work
hard and advertise successfully to keep it full. The size of hotel also
depends on the amount of room required by the owner for himself
and his family. Estate agents will often encourage you to buy a
larger, more expensive hotel than you can afford, so be wary. It is
all too easy to find yourself working mainly for the bank.

If you have doubts or queries on the subject of leasehold and
freehold property, consult your solicitor, who should be able to
advise you.

The condition of the hotel

A good survey will, of course, show up the main faults, but in the meantime you should do a survey of your own. Scrutinise the kitchen equipment, for the replacement of even one large item, such as a catering cooker or large freezer, can be expensive. Check the inventory of contents early on, so you can cost what may need replacing. You may find it impossible to supplement the existing china as the pattern is no longer made. Check on the condition of dining tables and chairs. Are the decorations in good order? Are the central heating and hot-water system adequate? Is the electrical wiring in a satisfactory condition?

In an existing hotel, fire-work may already be adequate; occasionally a hotel will change hands while fire-work is in progress, in which case ensure that the sale price enables you to complete this essential work, and that you know exactly what is involved before you exchange contracts. As long as the fire certificate has been applied for, you can receive paying guests. There is more about fire-work in Chapter 1.

Business structure

Many small businesses are run by the owner as a sole trader; the alternatives are partnerships or limited companies.

Sole trader
The owner trades alone, in his own name or under the name of the hotel. If the owner trades under the name of the hotel, his own name (and different address, if applicable) must be given on the hotel letterheads and all other business documents. He is self-employed, personally liable for all the debts of the business, and is personally entitled to all the profits. Personal liability means that personal assets can be sold by creditors to pay off any debts if the owner ever goes out of business. A self-employed trader pays Schedule D tax (see Chapter 3) and must register for value added tax when turnover exceeds £23,600 a year or £8000 or over in any quarter.

Partnership
It is best to approach with great caution the idea of going into business with friends or relations. Friction is caused when one is a workaholic and another on the lazy side; small vexations become exaggerated in the high season when you could be working a

14-hour day or more. In such stressful times, a unique combination of personalities is necessary for success.

Before going into partnership, and drawing up a formal agreement, discuss the matters which may give rise to controversy:

1. The responsibilities of each partner.
2. The proportion of capital to be contributed by each partner, and how the profits are to be divided. Bear in mind that one partner might contribute most of the work and the other most of the money.
3. How much remuneration will be drawn out of the business by each partner, and on what basis?
4. How will major decisions be made? If there prove to be insurmountable differences, what arbitration arrangements are there?
5. What arrangements will be made in the event of the death or incapacity of a partner for (a) the future of the business, and (b) the well-being of his dependants?
6. On what basis will a share of the business be valued in the event of the withdrawal or retirement of a partner?
7. What expenses can be charged to the business, such as cars (not used exclusively for business purposes) and telephone calls?

If you decide to proceed with a partnership, decisions on all the above points should be conveyed to your solicitor, who should be asked to draw up a partnership agreement for you. This applies even if the partnership consists of a husband and wife.

Sleeping partners
They have the same responsibility for all partnership debts as other partners, even in cases where they take no part in management and only play the role of backer in return for a share of the profits. Whatever arrangement you decide upon, see that it is put into the written agreement. Leave nothing to chance.

Private limited company
A limited company can be set up by any group of shareholders, one of whom must be a director. A company secretary is also required. The advantage of this arrangement is that if the company goes bankrupt, the shareholders' liability is limited to the face value of their shares; unless they have also given personal guarantees, their personal assets are safe. A limited company's articles of association set out its objects, and if you buy an existing company

'off the shelf', it is essential that the articles cover the business you plan to run under the name. Your solicitor can help you, or a company broker; it will cost in the region of £250 through a solicitor.

A limited company must keep accounts in a form specified by the Companies Acts; the accounts must be audited and an annual return in specified form made to Companies House. The directors are employed by the company and pay Schedule E income tax (see Chapter 3). Company profits are subject to corporation tax.

This form of incorporation is unlikely to apply to small hotels.

The hotel name

If you buy an existing hotel, consider the matter carefully before changing the name, as this might lose you the business that could accrue from existing directories in which the current name appears, and old clients may not recognise the place by the new name. Where a leasehold hotel is concerned, the owner's permission must be sought before a change is made.

Should a guest house proprietor wish to change the status of his establishment to that of a hotel, he should obtain a change of title form (from his solicitor) in order to do this. Providing there is no hotel of the same name already in the area, permission is usually granted.

Many people will book a hotel — other things being equal — because they like the sound of its name, so it is important to choose carefully. 'Grey Towers', however accurate and grand, will hint at grey days and may initially lose bookings. A strong picture should be projected by your name: 'Castleview Cottage Guest House' presents an immediate image. Names like 'Golden Meadow' and 'Summer Lodge' conjure up pictures of sunshine and lazy holidays in the country or by the sea. It is important to get it right.

Chapter 3

Finance and Accounting

Here we consider the financial aspects of running a hotel: finding the money in the first place, budgeting for the best use of it, and accounting for it later. Settling bills by customers is dealt with on page 75.

Raising capital

The cheapest money to use is your own, so you need to make a careful assessment of your assets — cash, savings, shares, life assurance, antiques or jewellery. Your house can be used to raise money in the form of a mortgage if you are not planning to sell it. All such items taken together can net a tidy sum, often enough to make a start with.

Private loans from friends, family and business acquaintances are investments by them in you; they will need to be paid the current interest rates and any such loans should be the subject of a legal agreement to avoid disagreement later. It should be made clear that such personal loans do not carry a say in the running of the business.

Banks are the commonest source of loans for small businesses. You will need to take your projections along and convince the manager of your ability to run a hotel; what will you say if he asks you, 'What could you do in the winter to augment your income if times prove difficult?' Many banks have special start-up loan schemes and will let you know what information they require before considering your application.

If you are taking over an existing business, the bank will certainly want to see the current year's audited accounts and a projection of anticipated takings in the following 12 months.

If you are buying an existing hotel and up-to-date audited accounts are supplied by the vendor and found to be satisfactory, a professional projection may be unnecessary. However, you will still need to work out a detailed business plan to support any application to borrow money.

A business proposal

This is the sort of prospectus you should draw up if you need to approach your bank manager or a finance house for a loan to launch your business. It should be carefully and neatly prepared, and contain all the relevant information about your proposed business, and may clarify your own ideas at the same time.

Give your name and address at the top, as the proposed proprietor. Then list the following:

- Details of the proposed business venture and its location.
- Information about the proprietor and a curriculum vitae with evidence of your ability to run the hotel.
- Full information about the premises, including present use, and whether your hotel will require planning permission; mention the existence or otherwise of parking space and any drinks licence.
- Your local research into the viability of a hotel there.
- What your financial requirements will be, (a) for setting up, and (b) for running the business during the first year. How much of this required capital will come from your own resources.
- Budget/projection for the first six months and the first year.
- Cash flow forecast for the same periods.
- Staffing requirement (or family help), whether full or part time.
- Personal and financial references for the proprietor.

Budget

To work out the budget, you will first need to decide the minimum weekly income that will meet your existing financial commitments, which might include mortgage, rates, gas, electricity, insurance, telephone, car, hire purchase, National Insurance (if already self-employed) and housekeeping expenses.

To this sum must be added a breakdown of the additional commitments incurred by starting up a hotel, such as loan repayments and charges, wages, water and sewerage charges, paladin waste container hire, food and drink (probably the largest outgoing sum after loan repayments), repairs and renewals, postage and stationery, TV rentals, advertising and publicity, subscriptions to hotel association(s), laundry, additional insurance (especially to cover loss of business), equipment hire, accountancy and legal fees. You will see that a lot of research is needed, and it involves estimating the projected business over the first 12 months.

Projection for a guest house

The professional projection below was drawn up for a young couple who were about to purchase a six-bedroomed, freehold guest house in 1980.

Basing your projected income on the exact bed space available is a chancy business. More often than not (except in the school holidays, at Easter, bank holidays and Christmas) only one — usually the double — bed is occupied for the greater part of the year in a family room (which can also contain either two bunk-beds, or two singles).

The pattern for holidays has changed enormously over the years. Where once the whole family packed buckets and spades and set off for a week or two by the sea in England, package holidays abroad now tempt many, and there are educational and adventure holidays for children. The two-week holiday has stretched to three and sometimes four weeks, enabling people to spread their breaks over the year.

The hotel comprises six bedrooms, plus a chalet at the rear. It is intended to let all six bedrooms, with the owners and their infant daughter occupying the chalet during peak periods.

As no reliable accounting figures are available on which to base our projection, we have used our experience from other hotels in the locality, plus information that the interested parties intend to use the benefit of trade connections, Saga Holidays (catering for senior citizens) and off-peak advertising to produce clientele during the close season.

The following notes should be read in conjunction with the projected account:

1. *Turnover (six letting bedrooms)*

	At full capacity £		Projected income £
Peak periods: 13 weeks @ 16 persons @ £63	13,104	(80%)	10,483
Early/late season: 13 weeks @ 16 persons @ £50	10,400	(30%)	3,120
Casual lettings: Winter/Easter etc			1,000
			14,603
		Say	£14,500

2. *Own board and residence*
   This is anticipated Inland Revenue adjustment for two adults and one infant child.
3. *Wages*
   The husband intends to be self-employed in the decorating trade and has informed us that he will provide all the cover necessary at meal times, thus removing the necessity to employ part-time staff.
4. *Repairs*
   Fire precaution work has been completed and we understand the hotel to be in an excellent state of repair. Nevertheless, our experience shows that an element of repair is necessary and we have reserved £750.
5. *Net cash surplus*
   This figure is after charging all basic living costs of the family including food, but before reserving for finance and depreciation.
   Anticipated income from self-employment has not been included although this will be an important factor to take into account when obtaining finance.

Projected account for the year ended 31 December 1981

	£	£
Turnover (Note 1)		14,500
Own board and residence (Note 2)		2,000
		16,500
Less: Overheads:		
Provisions 22½%	3,712	
Casual wages (Note 3)	nil	
Rates and water	600	
Light and heat	600	
Insurance	150	
Postage and stationery	100	
Publicity	300	
Telephone	100	
Motor	500	
Laundry and cleaning	350	
Professional	180	
Repairs and renewals (Note 4)	750	
Sundries	200	
		7,542
NET PROFIT		8,958
Less: Non-monetary item:		
Own board and residence		2,000
Net cash surplus (Note 5)		6,958

Except when fortunate enough to be booked solid with either small coach parties (or when sharing such parties with other hotels) your highest takings should occur during July and August; these are still the most popular months with most holiday-makers. The Easter and Christmas periods are good runners-up. Many hoteliers find May and June poor months for takings but, even here, it is difficult to generalise, for there are increasing numbers of social clubs holidaying in off-peak periods, and many senior citizens prefer a cooler climate (and less noisy holiday companions).

As far as the viability of any business is concerned, there is always room for improvement. Some concerns, once excellent, flounder because of partners' ill-health, loss of partners or genuine problems within the family. Often, such businesses have been run by the same family for many years so are well-established and worth looking out for.

Cash flow

A cash flow projection shows how much cash you will need at any given time, and is quite separate from profitability, which is assessed on an annual basis. A very profitable business could go broke because there was not enough cash in the till to meet bills by a certain date. Much depends on your financial status at the outset, the time of year you start operating, and the state of your bookings.

Opening your doors in November can be as bleak a prospect as the month itself; an already thriving business with healthy bookings laid on is an entirely different matter, but even then you have to stock up for Christmas. It stands to reason that, because of the climate, November, December (except for the Christmas period), January, February and March, are not all-time favourite months with the public in general. When commencing business in January or February, especially if running a family-type guest house or hotel, you can hold back the stocking of both freezer and food cupboards until nearer Easter (although the wise cook will take full advantage of the quieter periods and cook for the freezer). It does, naturally, all depend on how busy you anticipate trade will be.

The position would, naturally, be different should you decide to accommodate students, or take in residents and, if you plan a mainly commercial hotel, here again, you could be busier during the winter months.

Fortunately, banks familiar with the hotel business are only too aware of cash flow problems, and it is quite usual for them to allow a welcome overdraft facility whereby you can borrow an agreed sum over and above the arranged loan amount. If you are registered for VAT, keep a separate account for this tax to ensure you have it available when payment to HM Customs and Excise is due.

Keeping the books

It is essential to keep accounts; you must know where you stand financially at any time, and unless records are kept up to date, you may be unaware of problems until they overwhelm you. If the work is not done regularly, it takes more time in the long run, and a drawerful of bills and receipts is not helpful when you need to know how much you have in the bank to meet an unexpected demand. Always keep cheque book stubs filled in with the payee's name, amount, date of the account and the cash book reference number. Always make out a voucher for petty cash paid out if there is no receipt. Keep petty cash separate from takings and personal money.

If you have no accounting experience, it will be better to keep simple records, and ask your accountant to show you what is needed. Sole traders and partnerships must keep accounts for tax purposes. Limited companies are legally bound to keep accounts in a form specified in the Companies Acts. Your accountant will prepare the end of year accounts from the records you have kept.

Any VAT collected should be shown separately, as it is payable to HM Customs and Excise.

If you employ full-time staff from whom you deduct tax, National Insurance, etc, you will need to keep a wages book.

A trading account for a small hotel is shown below (1984).

	£	£
Receipts		16,947
Own accommodation		3.760
		20,707
Less: Purchases		4.114
GROSS PROFIT		16,593
OVERHEADS:		
Administration	2,893	
Establishment	4,725	
Financial	4,699	
Depreciation	894	13,211
NET PROFIT		3,382

Trading account

ADMINISTRATION	£
Postage and stationery	80
Motor expenses	375
Repairs and renewals	520
Telephone	599
TV rental	221
Advertising	679
Laundry	122
Sundry expenses	297
	2,893

ESTABLISHMENT	
Heat and light	999
Insurance	266
Rent	2,552
Rates	908
	4,725

FINANCIAL	
Loan interest	3,182
Hire purchase interest	420
Bank charges	749
Equipment hire	204
Accountancy	144
Legal fees	nil
	4,699

Schedule to trading account

Income tax and allowable business expenses

When the nature of your earnings changes, it is advisable to inform the local tax inspector, or to get your accountant to do so. It is also important, when moving from employee to full-time self-employed status, to inform the tax inspector, as the basis on which tax is paid changes. You will then be given some indication of allowable business expenses to be set off against your earnings for tax purposes. Broadly speaking, business expenses cover items 'wholly and exclusively incurred for the purposes of business'. However, there are items which are used partly for private and business purposes — your car or telephone, for instance. In such cases, only the proportion of expenditure that can directly be attributed to business use is chargeable against tax. Naturally, careful records of such use must be kept, and the extent must also be credible.

Schedule D tax is paid by sole traders and partnerships, and is assessed on income from trades, professions and vocations. It is paid on the preceding year's income. Sole traders and partnerships should keep proper accounts to know how profitable they are and to satisfy the Inland Revenue. Schedule E tax is payable on wages and salaries from employment. Limited companies pay corporation tax.

Where income from self-employment or even part-time employment differs from ordinary wage or salary-earning status, you are allowed, in assessing earnings, to charge any expenditure 'wholly and exclusively incurred' in carrying on your trade. Check with your accountant that all business expenses are claimed as entitled.

Some of the allowable business expenses are:

1. *The cost of goods bought for resale.*
2. *Running costs of your business.* Heating, lighting, rent, rates, telephone, postage, advertising, cleaning, repairs (not improvements of a capital nature), insurance and the use of special clothing.
3. *Wages and salaries.* Any sums paid to full-time or part-time employees. This does not include any salary you and your partners are taking from the business. However, a married man can pay his wife a salary where she is doing a reasonably convincing amount of work. This is an advantage if the wife's income from other sources is less than £2785 (1989/90) a year, the first slice of earnings being tax free.
4. *Travel.* Hotel and travelling expenses on business trips and in connection with soliciting business. In addition to such expenses, a claim can be made for the running cost of your car (including petrol), in proportion to the extent it is used for business purposes.
5. *Interest.* Interest on loans and overdrafts incurred wholly in connection with the business. This does not include interest on any money you or any partner have lent to the business.
6. *Hire and hire purchase.* Hiring and leasing charges and the hire element in hire purchase agreements (not the actual cost—this is a capital expense).
7. *Insurance.* Every kind of business insurance, including that taken out on behalf of employees, but excluding your own National Insurance contributions and premiums paid on your personal life insurance (such premiums are subject to separate personal tax relief).
8. *The VAT element in allowable business expenses.* This would include, for instance, VAT on petrol for your car. The VAT on the purchase of a motor car is allowable in all cases, since this cannot be reclaimed on your VAT return if you are registered.

9. *Certain legal and other professional fees.* Audit fees or court actions in connection with business (not penalties for breaking the law).
10. *Subscriptions to professional or trade bodies.*
11. *Gifts.* Business gifts costing up to £10 per recipient per year (excluding food, drinks, tobacco and vouchers exchangeable for goods). All gifts to employees are allowable; however, it should be remembered that employees may have to declare such gifts on their tax returns where the value is substantial.

This is not an exhaustive list of allowable business expenses, more a pertinent one: your accountant will advise and instruct wherever necessary.

Value added tax

VAT registration is applicable when your annual takings ceiling reaches £23,600 or £8000 or over in any quarter. Therefore, small guest houses and hotels, whose takings are under this ceiling, are exempt from paying VAT unless they plan to enlarge their premises and envisage a higher income in the next year. Full details are provided in the VAT handbook, available from HM Customs and Excise VAT offices.

Taxable turnover for VAT registration
The leaflet, *Should I be registered for VAT?*, which can be obtained from any local VAT office, explains taxable turnover and when a person carrying on a business is required to be registered for VAT. You should note that your taxable turnover will be less than your total turnover, if, for example, you run a small hotel or guest house and have guests who stay for longer than four weeks. This is because, when working out your taxable turnover you should exclude a part of the charge you make to guests who stay for longer than four weeks.

Your taxable turnover may well include any other taxable income that you may have.

Accommodation in hotels and guest houses is standard rated (currently 15 per cent); however, there is a reduction for guests staying for a continuous period of more than four weeks from the 29th day of their stay.

Long-stay arrangements — value for tax purposes

VAT must be accounted for on the full amount payable for accommodation facilities, meals and any extras, eg, drinks and tobacco for the first four weeks of a person's stay. Any service charge that you include in the bill is also taxable. After four weeks the amount subject to VAT is reduced for the remaining period by excluding the value of the accommodation. The reduced value must not be less than 20 per cent of the amount reckoned as due to the accommodation and facilities together, but if the value of the facilities is more than 20 per cent, tax is chargeable on that higher percentage. Tax is, of course, chargeable on the full amount attributable to meals, drinks, etc.

'Facilities' includes items such as cleaning, room service, laundry, porterage, TV, radio. It does not include meals or refreshments and extras, such as telephone calls, for which a separate charge is made. Tax is due on these charges in the normal way.

If a guest staying for more than four weeks spends weekends, holidays, etc, away from the accommodation, these are not regarded as breaks in the stay and you can continue to apply the reduced value from the 29th day of the overall stay. This might apply where an elderly resident goes to visit a relative or to people working away from home. A change of room during the guest's stay is not regarded as breaking the continuous period of letting.

A period for which a retaining fee is paid to reserve the accommodation during a temporary absence counts as a period of actual occupation. Such a retaining fee is regarded as payment for a continuing right to occupy the accommodation. It is taxable at the full or reduced rate, depending on whether the break comes before or after completion of the first 28 days' occupation. If the retaining fee after the 28 days is less than the amount by which your normal charge has been reduced for VAT purposes, then no tax is payable. Otherwise the fee must be apportioned.

Block lettings of accommodation

If you actually let a number of rooms to a tour operator for use by tour members, to a firm for use by its staff, visitors, etc, or to an airline company for use by its flight crews and passengers, reduced tax value provisions apply for the period of the letting in excess of four weeks, even if different persons occupy the rooms.

You cannot apply the reduced tax value to rooms which are booked or reserved for a period but are not taken up, that is actually let; nor to rooms which are booked for a period exceeding four weeks but which are taken up only now and then for periods of less than four weeks. In other words, you can use the reduced value provisions only when there is an actual and continuing single supply of accommodation for a period in excess of four weeks.

A supply begins on the day each room is made available and is charged for at the occupation rate, ie, from the day on which the accommodation is actually let. The reduced tax value will apply from the 29th day of letting of each room included in that supply. If the number of rooms occupied is subsequently increased, the reduced tax value will not apply until the 29th day of letting of each room. For a letting to be continuous it must be for successive full weeks (plus any odd days at the beginning or end). So, if you let accommodation to a tour operator from Thursdays to Mondays throughout a season, this would not be regarded as a single supply and you must account for tax on the full value of each of the successive supplies.

If there is any break in a block letting, that supply is ended and any subsequent supply must re-qualify. However, a supply will not be regarded as broken by, say, the overnight absence of an individual guest who reoccupies the accommodation the following day, eg, a member of a tour party taking an overnight excursion. Any normal letting of the room to someone else during the guest's overnight absence would not affect the position. Such a letting would not qualify for the reduced tax value.

Accommodation supplied to employees
If you supply accommodation in your hotel to your employees who pay for it in cash or by deduction from their wages, the sums paid include VAT, which you should account for on your VAT returns. The reduced value provisions may apply. If you provide the accommodation free, no tax is payable.

Forfeited deposits and cancellation charges
Non-taxable receipts. Where, for example, accommodation or a package holiday is not taken up, any forfeited deposit or other cancellation charge that is made is not a consideration for any supply and is therefore outside the scope of the tax.

Pensions

Everyone in the UK has some kind of state pension provision, but it is usually inadequate, and should be backed up by private savings schemes.

Self-employed people are eligible for tax relief on pension contributions, and pension funds are tax exempt, with the result that capital builds up more quickly than in other savings schemes. The investor can draw a lump sum on retirement, as well as a regular pension, and his dependants can have a lump sum if he dies before retirement age — benefits all denied by the state scheme. The main options are:

1. *Pension policy with profits.* Investing in a life assurance company, whereby your money is invested in stocks, shares, government securities or whatever. These profits are used to build up the tax-exempt pension fund you stand to get at the end of the contributable period. There is no time limit on this period but, of course, the more you contribute the greater the benefit will be and vice versa; you can choose to retire at any age between 60 and 75.

2. *Unit-linked pensions.* Unit-linked policies are a variant of unit trust investment. A regular monthly payment (or an outright purchase) is made to buy stocks and shares of a variety of investments through a fund, the managers of such companies being versed in the art of investing in the stock market.

Chapter 4
Professional Advice

If you plan to buy or open a hotel in the area in which you already live, it would be advisable to seek professional help locally. Your own bank manager will know your financial affairs, as will your accountant; a local solicitor will be more aware of local conditions regarding planning permission, licensing applications, and so on; local estate agents will know the property market in which you are interested.

Should you plan to start up in a new area, far from your present home, finding the right advice becomes slightly more tricky. You need someone who can provide the expertise you need *when* you want it; it's much easier for you if one person deals with your business, rather than an anonymous face in a large group practice, but you have to be sure he or she can meet your requirements: this applies equally to an accountant or a solicitor.

Banks

The local branch of your existing bank may be ideal for you, but if you want to borrow a large sum and the local bank manager proves reluctant, you will need to shop around once you have prepared your projections. Really small branches tend to have low discretionary loan ceilings. If your hotel is to be in a resort, the local banks are likely to be more conversant with the hotel business than would a suburban bank.

Bank managers in general are helpful individuals but, of course, are businessmen first. Their attitude depends, not only on your financial standing and the viability of your business plan, but also on the particular bank's policy and on the prevailing economic climate. Wherever possible, it is advisable to deal with the big High Street banks, and in some circumstances, three or four may have to be approached before a favourable response is obtained.

Solicitor

A solicitor is essential; he will advise you on how the law affects your business proposals, and act for you in any legal matter, particularly conveyancing if you are purchasing a property. These services are charged for, so every consultation will cost money; therefore, do a lot of homework yourself on your projected purchase or start-up plan before you get in touch with him.

He can quote an approximate price for handling the purchase of a property; he negotiates with the vendor's solicitor and undertakes local searches to ensure that the property is, in fact, the vendor's to sell, that there are no encumbrances on its use as a hotel, and that no development is planned nearby which would permit the council to purchase your property compulsorily. He draws up a contract for the vendor to sign and exchanges this with one signed by you, at which stage 10 per cent of the purchase price will be payable; completion (except in Scotland) takes place around four weeks later, when the balance falls due. If the purchase falls through for any reason, he will obviously charge you with all the expenses he has incurred on your behalf.

Surveyor

If you are buying a property, it is advisable to have a survey. If you need a mortgage, it will be obligatory. The estate agent or your solicitor could probably recommend a surveyor, or the proposed lender of the mortgage will nominate his own. Once again, a fee is payable, so check out the hotel thoroughly before getting in touch with a solicitor and surveyor. Your offer for a property should always be made subject to contract and subject to survey.

Accountant

An accountant can undertake *all* your accounting work for you — at a price. A solicitor or bank manager should be able to make recommendations about suitable firms.

Most small businesses arrange to keep their own weekly and/or monthly accounts, referring to an accountant when they have problems, and handing over the books to him at the end of the financial year for a professional audit to be made. The accountant will tell you what records he needs for this purpose.

Insurance

If you buy a hotel on a mortgage, the lender will nominate an

insurance company to provide cover for the structure. Once the
preliminaries of purchasing your hotel are dealt with, you should
approach a competent insurance agent. The vendor may recommend one. A meeting at the hotel might be useful to discuss your
needs; in your new circumstances, you will need more than personal, house and house contents insurance. A comprehensive policy will be required for:

1. Personal insurance (life and personal effects).
2. Hotel insurance. (If the property is leasehold, the landlord
   is likely to have it partially insured. Once you take over,
   you will probably be required to bear a proportion —
   possibly half — of the cost of such cover. This should be
   checked during purchase negotiations.)
3. Hotel contents.
4. Extra cover for accidents to guests, freezer spoilage, loss of
   business for specific reasons, fire, burglary, etc.

It is worth getting several quotations, and do query anything that
is not clear to you.

Hotel associations

There are many of these throughout the country, and they are
sources of guidance and information. Suppose, for example, that
you have moved to Blackpool from Bayswater, don't know a soul
in your neck of the woods and your drains need unbunging or the
central heating system breaks down. Whom to ask? Just which
engineer or maintenance man in the Yellow Pages? Such associations are just the bodies to turn to. Their annual fees are usually
quite modest, and they amply meet a need.

Quite apart from providing useful information, associations'
activities are multifarious. If your hotel is isolated, you will probably feel the need now and then to meet up with other hoteliers,
problems shared being problems halved. In the quieter seasons,
most associations arrange coffee mornings, talks and discussions
and occasional events, plus one or two yearly functions, such as a
dinner-dance and perhaps a coach trip to a place of interest.

Some areas operate a most useful 'early warning' chain system,
whereby participating hotels telephone (in alphabetical order) the
next 'link' of the chain, passing on a warning put out by the police.
In a large resort, where there is much to-ing and fro-ing and a high
density of hotels, there are obviously periodic incidents. Once

furnished with personal descriptions and car registration numbers (especially the latter) the hotelier feels at least partly equipped to deal with known undesirables.

Most associations publish a newspaper or booklet crammed with useful information and advertisements, which they circulate to members, and which covers anything from news of a new ring-road and the state of the parks, to cooking tips, anecdotes, members' letters, and lists of helpful names and addresses of tradespeople.

Chapter 5
Furnishing, Decor and Exterior

Personal taste being so varied, there can obviously be no hard and fast rules to follow when furnishing and decorating a hotel. It is only human nature to choose colour schemes and furnishing ideas which appeal to you personally, and here lies the danger!

First, ask yourself, and those close to you, if you have reasonable colour sense and coordination. If the answer is 'no', there will be no lack of offers of assistance. Well-wishers apart, there is an abundance of shops and stores with colour charts and sample coordinates; consult an expert to guide you if you are all at sea. Bookshops and chain-stores stock reasonably priced books and magazines on decor and furnishing, with helpful hints and photographed room settings; Marks and Spencers have an excellent range.

There's something to suit every pocket; the delightful Dolly Mixture and Laura Ashley ranges both produce fabrics and wallpapers, and Laura Ashley in particular has a vast array of coordinating accessories. Whether your fancy is for Regency stripes, cottagey chintzes, or something totally different, simple or exotic, there's something for everyone's taste.

In a family hotel it would be wise to keep colour schemes simple, bright and fairly light with, if possible, easy-care, washable surfaces (give a thought to sticky little fingers). More elaborate ideas and schemes can work beautifully but, generally speaking, the more work involved and the more intricate the decor, the higher the cost. If cost is immaterial, you can have a ball!

Whatever you decide on, give a thought to the changing seasons. Try to compensate inside for those grey, sunless days. Remember, white and pale blue can strike cold; green is restful; and pink, peachy and gold shades are warm and welcoming. If you do go in for dark or sludgy colours — which can be superb in the right setting and hotel — give a thought to the failing sight and uncertain tread of the older generation (bear them in mind, too, if considering low-slung seating and remember the difficulty of rising from it).

And consider the general overall 'welcoming' effect. When

choosing darker colours, good lighting is essential. 'Fire' lights provide only the bare minimum of light, and you will need to add one or two pools of extra light at night-time as a safety precaution, especially if you have any awkward corners or partly hidden sets of stairs. No one likes being sued! When replacing carpeting, consider a restrained pattern that won't show every footprint.

Do not under-estimate the effect of strategically placed mirrors — they reflect light and create a feeling of spaciousness and continuation. Little touches like pictures and plants, ornaments (even inexpensive ones) and flower arrangements, can transform an anonymous room into an attractive setting which welcomes your guests and invites them to relax. When putting finishing touches to your decor, remember necessary items like waste-bins in each room (including public rooms) and provide adequate ashtrays. Ask relatives and friends to save their magazines and paperbacks and pass them on; keeping the supply up to date can prove expensive.

If you have to decorate externally, shy away from garish colours. Keep schemes simple and inviting. If the brick or stone-work is in good condition, concentrate on giving a sparkling finish to wood frames and doors. And give thought to those extra 'wooing' touches, like gay awnings, hanging baskets, window-boxes and planted tubs. Subtle and imaginative lighting at dusk will attract more than the moths. Lamps in windows, external lanterns, concealed lighting behind porches and in reception areas, and 'spots' placed in your garden or grounds can combine to highlight your hotel appealingly. Higher electricity bills have to be considered as part of your advertising expenditure.

Entrance, hallway, reception area and stairs

It is important to create an immediate warm and welcoming impression. The initial impact felt when entering a hotel can set the tone for the remainder of the visitor's stay. It can be likened to two strangers meeting for the first time and feeling that certain rapport.

Front doors need to be carefully chosen. Solid doors are not a good idea, especially without glass inserts, side panels or windows; the proprietor cannot see *who* is without and the visitor cannot see *what* is within. A half-wood, half-glass door would perhaps be more suitable, or a good, strong glass door with a solid surround, avoiding the need for peepholes. Many hotels have two doors to retain heat, one more solid than the other, particularly where there is a glassed-in porch or entrance lobby. Whatever type door you choose, do see that the glass is always clean and the paint spruce.

On entering a hotel on a chilly day, one should be greeted by a waft of warm air (cold hotels are soon on the blacklist) and, on a warm day, wherever possible, by a fresher, cooler atmosphere. All odours must be banished. Imagine knowing immediately upon entry that brussels sprouts and cauliflower are on the night's menu, and that there are pets around!

Should you inherit or decide upon a patterned carpet, so much the better; plain carpeting is to be avoided in 'heavy traffic' areas, hallways and entrance lobbies in particular. Carpet should be of the best quality and highest grade affordable. It is quite usual for the same pattern to be extended throughout hallways, stairs, landings and passages. This continuity of design is more restful and pleasing to the eye than a series of uncoordinated sections of carpeting of varying colours and designs.

Carpet tiles are worth considering when replacing worn, hallway carpeting (especially when money for complete replacement is a problem). Such tiles can be chosen to tone in or contrast with existing stair carpet. Do make periodic checks on the wearing of stair carpet, from a safety as well as a cosmetic point of view.

Subtle lighting, an attractive flower arrangement or *objet d'art* (not expensive unless you have a very up-market hotel) set in front of a mirror in the hallway, combine to create a desirable effect. Spotlessly clean, bare halls are all very well, but may suggest austerity.

If the public telephone is situated in the hallway, the provision of a shelf or two for resting spectacles, phone books etc is important.

In a modest hotel, if the reception area is merely a small, sectioned-off space in the hall, dress it up a little by introducing a flower arrangement to tone in with the existing colour scheme, and place the visitors' book in a prominent position. (Very few small hotel reception desks are manned.) It is perhaps a good idea to have two guest books — one strictly a register of guests' names and addresses, the other for informal remarks. Most guests prefer to leave making comment in the guest book until the end of their stay ('the proof of the pudding' and all that). In larger hotels where reception desks are always manned, the procedure is more formal and registers are likely to contain little more than guests' names and addresses.

Keep furniture to a minimum in passages and on landings, for easy access to bedrooms, bathrooms and toilets, and to prevent accidents.

Suggested treatment of hall, stairs, landings and passageways
Light, warm-toned paint or wallpaper (whichever is your prefer-

ence) with complementary accessories (hard and soft furnishings) perhaps echoing one of the colours in the carpet. Hanging plants are an attractive way of picking out and highlighting any green in a carpet for instance. Select blending flower arrangements and toning prints for walls. Alternatively, use pristine white paintwork contrasting with warm wall and carpet tones. Whether the colour scheme is continued throughout the hall, stairs, landings and passages is purely a matter of personal taste, though it is generally considered pleasing.

Residents' lounge

Apart from a generally attractive appearance, comfortable seating is the most important factor when considering the furnishing of a lounge; relaxing there is, after all, the main aim. If the lounge is small, it is difficult to arrange seating as one would like, but do study the room and make the very best use of the space available. New loose covers can provide a temporary face-lift if existing suites and chairs leave something to be desired and, even where furniture is in good condition, loose covers are an admirable way of saving on wear and tear.

Most rooms have a central light, but for television viewing and to create a more relaxed atmosphere, well-placed lamps are ideal. Also see that there are sufficient coffee tables and side tables for coffee cups, ashtrays, reading matter and so on.

A snack tariff-board is necessary in the residents' lounge; do see that the food available (and times) and prices are clearly printed.

Most residents' lounges have a colour television set (larger hotels often provide sets in bedrooms as well). However, one set only can create problems. If you are fortunate enough to have two lounges, another television set may prevent discord.

Decorating suggestions

Where the lounge is virtually a continuation of the hall (sections of walls or doors removed) it is more flattering to both hall and lounge to continue the colour scheme or, at least, to keep it as harmonious as possible. However, where a door actually separates the lounge from the hall, a different colour scheme can be introduced (although, here again, harmony is the keynote). Seating should be chosen for comfort as well as looks.

A few points worth remembering: the lighter the ceiling colour, the higher the room appears; conversely, the darker the ceiling, the lower it seems; vertical stripes have a lengthening effect; lighter walls suggest spaciousness, while dark ones shrink a room's size (too large and overpowering a pattern also has this effect).

Dining-room

Many single people prefer to dine alone (remember *Separate Tables*?). This, of course, is not always possible, but it is most convenient if tables of various sizes are available in the dining-room. Round tables are appealing but not always suitable as they cannot be joined up to accommodate larger groups of people. When buying an already equipped and furnished hotel (which is the norm) one initially has to suffer what furniture is available. It is a great advantage if dining-room furniture is suitable and adequate, for the outlay of re-equipping and furnishing a room to seat, say, 15 to 30 people can be a heavy one. It is more than likely that both small and large tables will be available; where this is not so and larger parties are involved, two or three tables can be placed side by side to seat families and friends.

The placing of dining-room furniture has to be carefully thought out. Flexible seating is an obvious advantage, and care must be taken to space tables so that guests and staff have easy access (nothing is more embarrassing than a contest of elbows). Accidents happen when floor-space is too crammed with tables and chairs, and waiting on tables (a delicate, and at times, difficult task, even in favourable circumstances) can become a harrowing experience. The best possible use should be made of the available space and care taken in the placing of serving tables, trolleys, side-board etc for ease of serving and clearing.

Where table-cloths are used, they should be clean and attractive. Laundry can be a problem (and an expense) so consider the many drip-dry cloths available; they keep their crisp, fresh look wash after wash. Many hotels use a white, or pale cloth as a base, and choose another, smaller cloth of contrasting or toning colour, to go over the top, the effect being enhanced by matching napkins. Specially treated paper cloths can also be purchased — these have a deceptive finish and are most useful and reasonably priced. There are handy plastic cloths on the market too (some nasty, others soft and pliable); they are ideal for families when a quick wipe is all that is needed and have the added advantage of being machine-washable where necessary.

Polished tables are very attractive but hard work, and perhaps not the best choice for a family hotel. Tables with formica or similar surfaces are convenient and durable but cold in impact and can smack of a cafe, but this does depend on how you dress your table, of course. Simple flower arrangements — from a single rose, carnation or a spring posy, through to an artificial arrangement in winter — can enhance a table and make that little difference which counts for a lot.

When replacing dining-room furniture, remember that intricate carving is all very well but harbours the dust. Designs that are reasonably simple are so much easier to clean.

Dining-room decor

The decor of the dining-room depends on whether it is a separate room or an open-arched extension of another (perhaps the residents' lounge). If the latter, it would be better to continue colours chosen for the lounge. If the former, a separate colour scheme could be considered, but again, it would look attractive if tones echoed the colours chosen for the adjacent room. It depends on whether you have a preference for continuity (which looks spacious) or favour distinctly different schemes. Some hotels hint at Joseph's coat and sale-room bargains. It is a common problem when refurbishing and replacing, and not always easy to overcome when funds are short. However, subtlety does help when in doubt.

As eating is an all-important part of a visit or holiday, surroundings in which meals are served should be as conducive to their enjoyment as possible, and create a relaxing atmosphere. If the dining-room overlooks a pleasant garden or view, so much the better. If not, consider murals or groups of prints, a large painting or mirrored wall and more dramatic use of plants, or the introduction of subtly-lit niches highlighting flower arrangements or *objets d'art*. Lighting is particularly important in the dining-room, for too bright a light can be an immediate atmosphere-killer. There are a few alternatives: individual table lamps (though these can be tricky if much mobility is required), lamps set on sills, sideboards, serving tables and other strategic places, or candles in bottles or holders.

Bedrooms

The standards of comfort and facilities provided in a guest's bedroom should be the best you can afford. Some guests prefer the privacy of their own room to the social contact in a public lounge, so it is logical to make bedrooms as welcoming as possible. Comfortable easy-chairs — two in a double room wherever possible — are appreciated, and a firm, desirable mattress is, of course, of paramount importance (a surprising number of people suffer from back ailments).

Duvets are becoming more popular, and reduce the time spent on making beds. (Choose man-made fibres in a cotton cover for easy laundering; duck-feather fillings are all very well but cups of tea do get spilt on them from time to time.) Blankets, however, should be available as required for there are still many 'unconverted' with a preference for them. Any extras provided in guests' bedrooms depend, largely, on the tariff charged. It stands to reason that a charge of £12 or £14 per person per night for bed and breakfast could hardly include the provision of tissues or writing paper. Nevertheless, homely touches like a modest posy of flowers or a plant, and a ready supply of magazines and paperbacks are welcoming and help guests to relax and enjoy their stay.

Showers en suite are in demand and, where there is room to accommodate them, they save congestion in the bathroom and prove to be a great convenience to most. There is a vast range of shower units on the market and prices vary considerably, so there should be a model to suit everyone's pocket.

Bedroom decoration

It is as well, when considering the decoration of bedrooms, not to opt for blatantly feminine or masculine settings, for obvious reasons. And, when planning colour schemes, do take into account which direction the room faces. Pale blue and white have a cold or cool effect so, particularly where a bedroom faces north, are to be avoided. But even this ruling can be stood on its head when such cool colours are teamed up with vivid contrast colours and richly patterned prints.

In a room where there is a double bed which is placed against a wall (although this should be avoided if at all possible because of difficult access) consider over-the-bed lighting as it will be impossible to provide a lamp each side of the bed, unless it is wall-mounted. On occasion, one person sharing a double bed may wish to read while the other prefers to sleep, so a reading light is a minor but important factor to bear in mind.

Bathrooms

The cold, white, clean but sterile-looking bathroom suites have largely been replaced by coloured suites in a variety of shades. In the main, these are very attractive, although darker shades should be avoided for appearances' sake — they show every water mark, especially in hard-water areas, and need much elbow grease and care. However, when funds are short and you are stuck with a white suite in good condition, much can be done to cheer up the bathroom. Towelling or easy-care cotton curtains or blinds can be chosen to complement the colour of the carpet or floor covering and, when toning towels are introduced, plus one or two hanging plants, the overall effect can be most pleasing. Tiled walls are easy to clean, but where areas are only partially tiled, remaining walls or sections can be papered with washable papers for easy care when money is tight.

Cellars

The word 'cellar' is often subconsciously linked with dark deeds and flickering candles, and it is doubtful whether even the most innocent, spider-free cellar is the desirable place it could be. Many older hotel buildings have a cellar which, in many cases, could be made more use of. Sometimes cellars cover fairly large areas of neglected space, if not the whole foundations, and house little more than aged furniture, mysterious bundles and boxes, and long-forgotten cobwebbed household miscellania. Quite apart from its more usual role as a junk ground, when dry and clean, a cellar can be used to store drinks and bulky items, plus furniture overflow, for most hotels of any size find storage space an ever present problem.

However, depending on the cellar's general state of repair and dryness, and where the entrance or exit is situated, much can be done to put it to even better use. Where finances are available to carry out a necessary face-lift, or repairs and decorations, a good cellar can be turned into an atmospheric bar room or a games cum play room for children.

Particularly when converted into an attractive bar room, a once dreary cellar could bring in welcome takings. When deciding on such a scheme, you will need to give the matter careful thought and planning to do it justice and make the best possible use of available space. Here, decor is vitally important and all manner of ideas and themes could be employed, from a nautical flavour to favouring the popular 'olde worlde' concept. Subtle lighting is as important as decor to enhance the chosen setting, so consider as many alternatives as you can.

Should you opt for a games room, all the more obvious and favoured facilities spring to mind, ie, provision of darts board (positioned in a safe place) pool/snooker table (enormously popular at present), a table-tennis table, card tables, a games area; a juke-box may also be considered and/or a drinks machine (this will free you for other duties).

Where a children's play room is being planned (it may be that the bar room is already well-established and an attractive feature in another part of the hotel), lighten up the area with gay, vivid or pastel colours, murals or simple stick-on motifs and cartoon characters. Even if the play room is little more than a sparsely furnished area to begin with, the space itself will appeal to the energetic youngster. (Suitable flooring, such as soft washable tiles, cork or carpet tiles, or a heavy-duty haircord or similar finish should be used.) Where there is only one entrance, the safety factor is there too, and parents could relax in the knowledge that their youngsters are 'penned up'.

Play room

It is doubtful whether many smaller hotel buildings can accommodate a specific play room (even the smallest room is sorely needed to boost income). However, where there is no cellar space, some alternative provision can usually be made. Even a simple toy-box or a few playthings provided in any available space — however small — or a corner of the garden set aside as a playground, would be useful. Small considerations such as these are appreciated when the hotel is geared more to entertaining the family.

Heating

A central-heating system may already be installed in the hotel of your choice, be it solid fuel, gas or electric. If it is in good running order and suitable for your needs, count it as a bonus. Should this not be the case, call in a recommended heating engineer and discuss your requirements. Although a sound central heating system is initially expensive to install, it is certainly worth it in the long run to have a constant, regular flow of warm air when required. Individual gas fires and electric heaters are all very well in their way, but an all-embracing system is usually preferable. Comparative running costs will need to be discussed with the heating expert. (At the time of writing, gas central heating running costs may have the edge.) Free-standing electric heaters should be avoided where possible due to high running costs, and paraffin heaters are too much of a fire risk when unattended, apart from causing respiratory problems for some. Avoid heat loss where possible to keep the bills down.

Lighting

Although general lighting has been mentioned, the whole subject of artificial lighting is worth exploring in more detail. There are those who don't give the correct or required wattage in any given situation a second thought, which is a pity. Apart from fulfilling specific needs, ie, reading, television viewing, sewing etc, too dim a light can be as harmful to the atmosphere as that which is too bright. Especially when the general decor is not as bright as it might be, low-wattage lighting can cast an air of gloom. Conversely, one should avoid a 'Crystal Palace' effect — not only is it too dazzling for the eye, it is also harmful for the pocket. Even in daytime, particularly when there is little sunshine, there is sometimes a need for soft pools of light. A small lamp may be all that is needed.

It is worth mentioning that different colour schemes have adverse or flattering effects on lighting; pink — although a warm colour — is a bad light reflector, as is green, whereas cream and, of course, white are very good reflectors of light.

Take a new look at your hotel

An interesting exercise — and if one is honest, beneficial for passing trade — would be to evaluate your hotel from the guest's point of view. A lot can be learned by working your way through the following checklist once a year.

1. *The hotel facade*
   What image does it present?
   Is it perhaps a little seedy?
   Is it a little on the bare, bleak or garish side?
   Does it beckon warmly?

2. *Hotel signs*
   Is the hotel sign clearly visible from all directions?
   Is one sign sufficient? (When situated on a corner, or detached, three hotel signs may be desirable for maximum impact.)
   Have you an illuminated sign for evening display? (If not, do consider one: although expensive they are a vital part of advertising.)

3. *Visibility of hotel entrance, and attractiveness of lighting*
   Is your main hotel entrance partly obscured by a tree, overgrown bushes or hedges?
   Is your hotel entrance lobby/hallway/reception area lit during the daytime? (Many unlit interiors appear gloomy in daylight when viewed from outside. Some form of lighting should be introduced; this need only be a lamp or strip-light.)

4. *If you are situated in a row of terraced or semi-detached hotels:*
   Does your hotel stand out? If not, why not?
   List what you would look for or be impressed by if cruising by in a car:
   (a) Overall welcoming impression.
   (b) General condition and spruceness of hotel: brickwork/woodwork/garden/forecourt.
   (c) Imaginative treatment, eg blinds or awnings, window boxes, tubs, flowers and so on.
   (d) A certain architectural appeal which may give an edge over neighbouring hotels.
   (e) Neat, clean curtains and clean windows.
   (f) Particularly attractive garden, umbrellaed tables, and chairs.
   (g) And, at night, subtle and imaginative lighting.

   If you passed the 'first impression' test, the potential guest will then be ringing your bell.

5. *Entrance hall/reception areas*
   Is the overall effect of these areas welcoming and pleasing?
   Is the tariff board in a good position for easy reading and recognition?
   Is your hall/reception area too austere or cluttered?

6. *Rooms*
   (a) Residents' lounge:
       Does it have a pleasing atmosphere?
       Invite you to relax?
   (b) Dining-room:
       Are table-cloths clean and attractive?
       Does the general appearance beckon?
       Are there flowers (artificial or real) on the tables?
   (c) Bedrooms:
       Do they strike cold or warm?
       Do they seem damp or smell musty?

Is furniture 'out-of-ark'/reasonable and adequate/
attractive?
Are towels and other linen clean?
Is the bed comfortable, and are the sheets cotton?
(Nylon sheets are, in the main, very unpopular!)
Has enough thought been given to overall effect?
(d) Toilets/bathrooms:
Are they clean?
Are they imaginatively decorated? (Toilets/bathrooms
do not have to *appear* sterile.)

The exercise isn't over yet . . . Stroll around your hotel; that isn't —
heaven forbid — a cobweb in the corner, is it? Are ashtrays emptied
regularly? Is your hotel warm enough in winter; well ventilated in
summer? What sort of atmosphere does it have? This may be a
tricky question to answer, for atmosphere is sometimes difficult to
define. However, if a hotel is old, well-preserved, furnished
appropriately, thoughtfully decorated, and punctuated by those
touches which make just that difference, one could claim it had an
'old-world charm and a homely atmosphere'. If, however, the
proprietors are too reserved and formal, the atmosphere can be
diluted to its detriment! On the other hand, of course, a bright,
modern hotel, tastefully decorated and furnished has much appeal
and can have a 'lively, modern atmosphere', perhaps appealing
more to a younger age group (although it can be a mistake to
categorise). 'It's all very well pigeonholing hotels,' you may say,
'but mine is neither one thing nor the other!' A good point. Here
again, the hotel can be treated imaginatively and revitalised where
necessary. Introduce one or two interesting features: a mirrored
wall perhaps? A new fireplace in the guests' lounge? A mural in the
dining-room? A desirable atmosphere can be created when these
are allied to other, more enigmatic, ingredients. Some folk do seem
to have more of a knack at creating atmosphere than others.

A few other, random, questions
Is drawer and hanging space in the bedrooms adequate?
Is the notice regarding vacating rooms and methods of settling
bills clearly printed and well placed?
Is there too much or too little display material in the reception
area?
Are 'Fire' notices clearly printed and prominently displayed in
guests' rooms?
Are all guests conversant with fire drill?

No doubt there are many more questions that can be added to the list; the more you can think of, answer and take heed of, the better.

Summing up

You may already be aware of shortcomings in your hotel's appearance, facilities or attractiveness but are unable, for financial reasons, to take immediate positive action about all of them; however, they are worth tackling one at a time. Once you have implemented improvements, recognition of your efforts will be reflected in increased passing trade.

Chapter 6
The Kitchen

The kitchen is the most important room in the hotel; the very heart if you like. Its planning and layout are, therefore, critical. Existing kitchens do not always fulfil one's needs; some are badly designed — if planned at all. Much of the day, unless a chef is employed, will be spent in the kitchen, so it is vital to your mental and physical well-being that much-used appliances, utensils, ingredients etc are grouped and positioned to the best advantage. Walking 10 to 20 feet unnecessarily innumerable times a day — especially on a concrete-based floor — is a recipe for back-ache and leg-ache, not to mention the time-wasting involved.

Hotel kitchens present different images for different people. They can be imagined as streamlined, stainless-steel affairs — all bustling efficiency that hints at assembly-line precision — or esoteric dens, out of the depths of which emerge who knows what gastronomic delights. In truth, no doubt, the majority hover somewhere between the two.

The size of the kitchen is not always indicative of the size of the hotel; occasionally, even where the building provides up to 12 bedrooms and reasonably-sized public rooms, kitchen dimensions are surprisingly small in comparison. Many hotels still suffer poky kitchens, so ensure that you are satisfied with it when purchasing your hotel. Alterations on a large scale can be costly, although occasionally it is simply a matter of rearranging appliances to work to better advantage and maximise efficiency (some are more gifted than others in planning for their needs). It is no easy matter to come across the 'ideal kitchen'. Keep floors dry and slip-proof if possible, and keep a fire extinguisher handy. Cooking fires should be smothered in a cloth or rug, rather than having water thrown over them.

Sinks and work surfaces

Larger hotels have the advantage in that preparation rooms are usually adjacent to kitchens and often provide an extra sink or two. These are mostly stainless steel, some being deeper than others, therefore having a larger capacity for washing/soaking bulkier items, such as large saucepans and baking tins. Where there is an extra sink close at hand, it eases the work-load and human bustle in the kitchen itself. Also, such sinks can be used specifically for washing larger quantities of fresh vegetables etc where necessary. Unfortunately, too few small hotels are fitted with such amenities, and all too often, a modest-sized sink has to cope with much and work overtime. If you are contemplating improvements, changes or actual extensions, a double sink is well worth the extra expense involved.

The siting of work surfaces is vital to the smooth running of the whole catering process and the staff's well-being. Work surfaces need to be uncluttered and made of strong, impervious and durable material. Where once kitchen tables were all made of plain, unadulterated wood, and scrubbed daily by an under-kitchen maid, most modern kitchens have work-tops made of formica or a similar strong and durable material. A few of the larger, old hotels may still proudly boast a marble work surface or two, but there is more evidence of stainless steel, moulded and formica-type work-tops.

The correct height for units, sinks, tables etc is important to prevent back-strain; this should be borne in mind when re-equipping kitchens. An 'island', consisting of a box-shaped arrangement, providing a work-top and shelves underneath, also drawers and cupboards, where there is room, can be most convenient. Existing tables can also be boxed in to maximise usage of all available space (especially valuable in the smaller kitchen) and shelving at eye-level and higher can accommodate many useful items.

The kitchen layout shown opposite is not so much a recommended example of how a kitchen should be planned, but more a rough guide and an indication of how the layout of even a simple, smallish kitchen can work fairly well. As it is unlikely that many of the kitchens in smaller establishments are architecturally planned and laid out, this may be helpful.

All available space has been used to maximum advantage; practically all eye-level areas have been equipped with cupboards and much-needed shelving. Easy access both into and out of the dining-room is obvious (the waste disposal bin can be placed near the back door for convenience). Sturdy, hinged drop-leaf shelves are useful when space is at a premium and every seat is taken. The immediate need between courses is free surfaces near a dishwasher or sink for stacking and disposing of dishes. The sink and warming cabinet are situated either side of the cooker for ease of preparation,

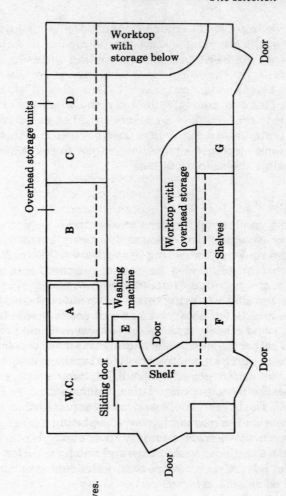

Worktop with storage below

Door

Overhead storage units

D

C

B

A

Worktop with overhead storage

G

Shelves

Washing machine

E

Door

F

W.C.

Sliding door

Shelf

Door

Door

A   Dishwasher
B   Sink and drainers
C   Gas cooker
D   Hot cupboard
E   Mobile fryer
F   Freezer
G   Refrigerator

Broken lines indicate
overhead units or shelves.

conveying of food to the cooker and for plating up of meals (the flat top of the warming cabinet can be used as a work surface or the cabinet can be eased under an existing work-top to save space, if necessary). The refrigerator and freezer are also positioned for easy access and placed near a 'table-cupboard' with suitable work-top. This is, of course, a 'limited menu' kitchen. Where an à la carte table is concerned, two cookers would be essential. Keep kitchen units simple in design where possible; also give thought to flooring — some older properties have stone floors, which is the worst possible choice for your legs.

Cookers

Many small hotel kitchens have either a very large catering-size stove, sporting two ovens and six ring burners, or two conventional cookers. Extra ring burners are so useful for the mornings when requests arrive for boiled, poached, scrambled and fried eggs, and porridge. It does happen. Fried eggs in particular don't take too kindly to being thrust into a hot cupboard for long periods (one misguided hotelier I know of cooks breakfast last thing at night and reheats it in his microwave oven next morning).

Whether a cooker is electric or gas is a matter of personal choice; where a purchased hotel is provided with an adequate cooker, then the problem is already solved! For catering purposes gas is perhaps the more popular choice, being instant and easily controllable. Each year, more and more sophisticated cooking ranges appear on the market; however, replacing a large, catering stove, or even the domestic variety, is a costly business. As with all modern equipment, the range and finish vary a lot, so the choice is wide; advertising newspapers, hotel contents' sales inventories and so on should be studied.

The microwave oven

From the point of view of convenience, particularly when serving hot snacks, the microwave oven heats pre-cooked foods quickly and efficiently. These appliances are becoming cheaper and more popular, and there are now models available in which certain dishes can be browned, adding to eye appeal.

The pressure cooker

The pressure cooker in our kitchen received many an appreciative pat. It can be relied upon to preserve flavour, cook quickly and efficiently, and where necessary, deal with several different vegetables at the same time. Although most types are similar, there are various makes on the market to choose from, all well-tested and reliable.

Deep fat fryer

Here again, there are several types of fryer; a small, free-standing model which can be placed on top of existing work-tops (this is handy when the menu is split and only a few portions of fried food are required); single, double or triple stainless-steel containers which can be conveniently positioned alongside your stove, or a larger, free-standing type which can be mounted on castors for easy use and storage. These models are perfect for cooking many dishes, from potato croquettes to french fries.

The hot cupboard

Where staff are thin on the ground, and therefore time is precious, the hot cupboard really is a useful piece of equipment. Life in the kitchen is so much more tolerable when meals can be plated up in advance — though timing here is critical. There are several types of hot cupboard made in various sizes to fit in with existing appliances and work-tops. Most of them are thermostatically controlled and made in stainless steel. As when replacing other kitchen equipment, check out all the usual outlets for second-hand bargains; there are many to be found.

Freezer and refrigerator

Freezers are commonplace nowadays, and a boon, particularly to the caterer. One is likely to be inadequate, so if only one is already installed, you would do well to invest in a second. Apart from the freezer section of a refrigerator for smaller items — a large refrigerator is a must — there are two main types of freezers to consider: the chest model (which uses less electricity), or the upright type. For ease of access and convenience, one freezer is best sited close to much-used appliances and is therefore best stocked with frozen items needed from day to day. The second freezer can be sited further away from the kitchen, particularly if the kitchen is small. This can be stocked with standby items or products with a longer shelf life, and also used when preparing items for freezing in the kitchen. It is helpful to keep a list close to both freezers itemising the products within so that replacement can be effected where

necessary. Insurance cover for freezers is essential, especially for
replacement of ruined contents.

General cooking utensils

Stainless steel and aluminium ware is commonly used in hotel
kitchens (with perhaps a few enamel 'left overs'). Copper containers are also used, but copper is expensive and requires more
attention and upkeep. A variety of saucepans is obviously needed
but, of course, the larger pans will be used with more frequency.
Frying pans, too, will be required. Treated surfaces (teflon etc) of
both saucepans and frying pans are excellent when used with
respect — and when catering for smaller parties — but for sheer
durability stainless steel is more reliable. Special omelette pans
are essential, and roasting tins and trays another consideration
(the use of foil here aids oven cleaning). Ensure that pans are the
correct depth to accommodate the size and volume of contents.
Grids and trays are most useful when cooking on top of the stove,
especially when frying smaller quantities, as the oven can be used
as a hot cupboard, and food to be kept warm for a short period
placed on a grid over the tray to assist fat drainage.

A cool surface is required when making pastry, and cold marble
is ideal. Marble pastry blocks and rolling pins have recently made
a welcome reappearance and are available in most of the larger
stores and specialised catering shops. Keep a look-out for marble-
topped tables in antique and bric-à-brac shops. (If space is short,
remove the legs and place the marble slab on a portion of an
existing work surface.)

Meat slicer and food mixer

There are still cooks who prefer to prepare everything by hand,
although the betting is that they're in the minority. For most of us,
food mixers and meat slicers are both a great help and time saving.
There are those with a knack of slicing meat, but however deft one
is with the knife, there are occasions when certain joints behave
perversely. There is the added danger of cutting uneconomical
slices. Uniformity of shape, size and weight is a requirement when
catering, and evenly sliced portions are more pleasing to the eye
than pieces of various shapes and sizes.

A food mixer that chops, whips, mixes and performs other minor
tasks in seconds is a boon to the caterer. More sophisticated
functions are continually being added to the basic design.

Always be wary when using food mixers, meat slicers, electric knives, etc. Although modern equipment incorporates safety devices, accidents can still happen all too quickly when time is short (and when you are over-familiar with equipment and off-guard).

The automatic toaster

Most hotel kitchen cookers have a large grill which is perfect for toasting bread, buns etc in quantity. However, there are occasions when only a few slices are required, and others when there is an extra-heavy demand. In both cases, the automatic toaster will help out; also when toast is required for serving with pâté, and the stove is heavily laden. Free-standing toasters are also movable, and can be re-sited. Most models are similar in design, and there are many makes, colours and finishes to choose from.

Knives and chopping boards

It is said that sharp knives are, in the long run, the best way of preventing accidents; too often, one hacks, saws or chops with a blunt knife, which can easily lead to bloodshed. Ensure that knives are sharpened regularly and kept in a *safe* place. Chopping boards or blocks are sometimes inadequate affairs. Shop around for an ample one — there are numerous and varied types on the market — or have one specially made. The good old butcher's block of yesteryear too is to be envied (except from the scrubbing angle).

The potato peeler

Potato peeling is a dirty and irksome chore, disliked by most and very time-consuming. An electric potato peeler is therefore a godsend when catering for many people. Such machines can cope with several pounds at one time, making the task of checking for remaining 'eyes' far less formidable. When business is slacker, double the quantities of potatoes prepared at any one time — the unused portion can then be kept immersed in cold water for the next day's use (save time wherever possible).

It is worth visiting a catering equipment store (even if there is no present intention of buying) to examine just what equipment is available. As technical strides are made, equipment of all types becomes more and more sophisticated and efficient, and it is worth knowing what modern technology is producing, and comparing it, pricewise and efficiency-wise, with the more familiar types of equipment on sale. Then, if business is successful and sights have been set on a particular item, it may be well worth buying.

Measuring scales

A measuring scale in your kitchen is essential. Wall-mounted types are convenient, needing no other space for their housing and being close to hand. There are many types on the market; it is all a matter of personal taste. Even the most adept cook needs to weigh ingredients from time to time and, although daily used vegetables and more commonly used ingredients can be judged, more or less, without weighing, certain recipes call for more precise measurements, which to ignore would be foolhardy and could result in a disappointing dish.

Smaller cooking aids, such as strainers, soup ladles, spoons, spatulas and so on should be grouped as near to the scene of action as possible; next to the cooker and adjacent work surfaces is usually the most convenient place. This also saves much to-ing and fro-ing and possible collisions with staff.

The kitchen water boiler

Not every small hotel is fortunate enough to own (or have the room for) a machine which provides constant boiling water when needed for tea, coffee or other use. Such machines are run by either gas or electricity although electricity may have the edge for, while slightly more expensive to run than gas, the appliances are cleaner. Water boilers are made in various sizes and, even when a business is on the small side, worth procuring where there is room; a small model could always be positioned on an existing work-top. The alternative, of course, is one or more large kettles. Some of the older types can be very heavy and, depending on their siting for ease of pouring, are difficult to handle and lift comfortably and, once again, great care should be taken; burns and scalds can happen in a second. Where kettles are over-heavy and cumbersome, replace them forthwith.

Dish-washing machine

Although essential in larger hotels, these machines can be controversial. There are those who wouldn't be without one for the world, while others argue that, by the time food particles are rinsed off and dishes stacked, it is hardly worth the bother. A lot depends on whether *you* have to do the washing up continually. If the initial outlay and running costs are compared with employing a part-time *plongeur* over a long period, the machine will probably be decided upon. Larger, rather than smaller, types are worth considering as, all too often, the smaller model just doesn't cover your needs.

Hiring

Be wary when hiring machines. Apart from the initial fee sometimes charged, the hirer is often held totally responsible for the machine's maintenance and ultimate delivery back to its source once the hiring period ceases. Read the small print in contracts carefully. Once signed, such agreements can be a millstone around your neck. Tot up what the initial fee (if any) and two years' payments amount to, and it could well prove more economical to purchase a brand new machine on credit, or a guaranteed second-hand model.

Cake tins

There is a huge range of such tins on the market, many now coated with convenient, non-stick surfaces (which again need careful handling and washing). If used as instructed, such tins are an aid when time, and sometimes patience, is short. Batches of cakes of all sizes can be made and cooled more speedily because of ease of removal. How varied a range of cake tins you wish to carry will depend on personal taste, demand, and just what proportion of the baking you intend to be home made.

Extra storage space

When there is a small room, area or cupboard set apart which is deemed suitable for the storing of bulkier items and products with a long life expectancy (residue of bulk buying etc) much care should be taken to ensure that such areas are kept clean, dry and checked for possible intrusion of vermin. When dry and clean, sheds, outbuildings and cellars can be ideal storage places. Tinned and bottled products, strongly boxed items and non-perishables (cleaning materials, toiletries and so on) can be safely housed, provided stringent checks are made on slow-moving stock. Keep a stock list on the door of such a place to assist when time is short; items removed can be crossed off, giving a clear indication of the balance remaining when reordering.

Food with a shorter shelf-life should, of course, be stored close at hand where regular inspections can be made easily.

Where store-rooms and outbuildings are accessible to the public, it would be wise to keep them securely locked, particularly when sited outside the hotel.

Hygiene

Although general cleaning is a mixture of hard work and common sense, there are areas where many have been tried and found wanting. Periodic checks are made by Health Inspectors and, in the main, the kitchen is their first port of call. Particular note is taken of preparation surfaces and their state, the appearance of the cooker and refrigerator, also cutlery and crockery. Cracked or broken floor covering gets the thumbs down sign as do cupboards and shelves neglected for too long, and dirty tiling around sinks. All of this is a comfort to the public. However, the few erring parties who escape the net are usually caught and reprimanded eventually. Hygiene courses are a good idea, for hygiene is a broader subject than you may imagine and many tips can be picked up. Such courses are run in many areas.

Disposal of rubbish

When every seat in the dining-room is taken, you can bet your bottom dollar that the paladin (described below) will be overloaded, and that the immediate disposal of daily waste from dining-room and kitchen will be a problem. However, paladins are capacious, the main problem being the tide of mounting waste while you are involved elsewhere during meal times. A carefully sited over-sized bin, box or plastic bin-liner, is probably the easiest way to prevent your kitchen becoming ankle-deep in egg shells, bacon rinds and general kitchen waste. When the hectic meal-time is over, it is then a simple matter to transfer any rubbish to the paladin outside.

The paladin is a large, cylindrical metallic bin on castors — ideal for holding large amounts of waste material. Paladins are usually emptied once a week in most areas. Local town halls or council contractors issue an invoice for supplying and emptying them — the hire charge being £70 per year plus £144.96 for emptying (1989). Bottles can be disposed of in these containers where necessary, but it is preferable to dispose of empty bottles in a bottle-bank if there is one nearby. See page 79 regarding beer bottles.

Chapter 7
Daily Operation of the Hotel

It is, of course, essential to introduce some semblance of order and routine into the running of even the smallest guest house or hotel.

An average day

Breaking down the usual chores in an average family hotel, the following is a typical example of a day when there are a dozen guests staying.

Partner 1. Having revived oneself, repair to kitchen to prepare and cook breakfast for 12 persons (someone *would* want porridge). Serve. Wash up or stack dishes in washing-up machine; dry and put away. Wipe down surfaces; clean cooker. Answer the phone (perhaps twice). Have own breakfast. Check food cupboards and freezer (or lists); make out shopping list. Answer door and deal with salesman/guest. Sell map/postcard to guest; indulge in small-talk or give directions. Replace faulty light-bulb (on second floor, of course). Deal with other, minor necessary tasks. Peel potatoes, prepare other vegetables, fish/meat or whatever. Stop for lunch. Motorised shopping trip. Return and put away purchases. Prepare and serve one or two trays of afternoon tea with biscuits, cakes, or serve a lager/sherry or two. Prepare and cook evening meal; repeat morning procedure. Pause to wonder why fitting of wheels on soles of feet wasn't obligatory at birth. Eat own meal (in between showing member of public a room). Serve drinks in bar; indulge in more small-talk. Generally play role of 'mein host', check hi-fi tapes, wash glasses, serve nuts, crisps and more drinks. Close bar, check takings, wash remaining glasses, empty ashtrays. Batten down the hatches, check there is sufficient, unfrozen bacon and bread for breakfast (to prevent oneself leaping out of bed at 4 am like a scalded cat).

With luck, you may just beat the chimes of midnight (no bets taken). On some occasions, there are numerous interruptions; on others, none. Then there is the car to clean and check, vegetables to weigh, blanch and freeze, the garden to take care of, extra rubbish to be disposed of etc. No two days will be exactly the same.

Partner 2. Having withstood the shock of morning, proceed to make early morning tea for six souls languishing in their beds (does Mrs C take sugar/biscuits?). Check tables for breakfast. Check and tidy guests' lounge, hall etc. Prepare starter and assemble toast-racks, tea-pots, and so on. Serve breakfast (smiling); clear tables, wipe sauce-bottle tops, check marmalade, sugar. Make up any flasks/packs of sandwiches required. Have breakfast. Throw washing in machine. Tidy, dust and vacuum dining-room. When guests have departed, 'do' their rooms — changing linen where necessary, replenishing soap/bin-liners, and so forth. Clean showers, loos and bathroom(s). Sit on stairs for coffee break. Hang out washing. Inspect, dust and vacuum stairs, landings, hallway. Pause to rebuff enthusiastic salesman at door. Show would-be guest a room. Clean remainder of hotel where necessary — including own accommodation. (Seeing to one's own brood has to be dovetailed between hotel duties, of course. If they are older, and at school or work, so much the better!) Return to kitchen to sweep and clear up (if necessary) after partner. Lunch break. Deal with bookings, type replies to letters and send off tariffs. Dovetail with partner in the serving of afternoon teas where necessary. Prepare hors-d'oeuvres and desserts; lay tables. Refresh/replenish flowers. Iron or do accounts. Post letters; do spot of gardening. Answer door/phone and generally see to guests' needs. Bring in washing. Serve dinner; clear tables. Own dinner-break. (See to offspring.) Dovetail with partner on bar duties and guests' needs. When the last guest departs for bed (if dining-room doubles as bar-room) lay tables for morning. Remember *not* to lock front door.

Telephoned bookings

Where a person is merely enquiring about tariff, facilities and dates available, dealing with such a call is routine and unlikely to involve any problems. Occasionally, someone will request more specific details, require a special diet, or whatever, and it is simple enough to note — in *pencil* in the booking book against the appropriate date for which the booking is required — just what is involved. Make sure you have *all* necessary information, such as details of the diet. Perhaps a shower room was requested; whether, for reason of age (either very old or young) mention was made of a reduction. The last item is important, as much embarrassment can be caused if a note is not made of any such arrangement. Even where a person promises to send a deposit and doesn't require further information, it is perhaps wise to write a simple letter, concluding on the lines, 'Looking forward to hearing from you.' Some are well-intentioned but extremely tardy when it comes to confirmations and deposits.

'On-the-spot' bookings can be more ticklish, and you have to be quick off the mark not to lose an 'iffy' booking. Just suppose it is May — your tariff is fixed at £85 for bed, breakfast and evening meal, inclusive — and, although the area is generally quiet, you have only two double rooms left. The telephone rings: 'I have seen your advertisement and would like to book two double rooms — we are already in the area ... '. You reply that you do indeed have two double rooms — very nice rooms, with a view of the sea. 'The only problem is,' the voice continues, 'we are old-age pensioners and can't really afford £85. Could you make a reduction?' You hesitate for a second, oh of course you can. 'Certainly,' you hear yourself saying, 'How does £79 sound? May I have your name and address? I see, you'll be along round about 5pm.' Ten minutes later, two 'doubles' knock on the door! Ah well, you've pleased two other old souls, and who's to say that more business won't accumulate from that booking. Just a point in conclusion; suppose the two couples who booked by telephone (there's no deposit remember) fail to appear ... Thankfully, the case doesn't occur every week, or month, but such situations do arise. It can be a dilemma but must be regarded as one of the occasional pitfalls of the trade.

Apart from keeping a reservations book, which is in effect a dated diary of your bookings, a wall chart is a good idea, especially if conveniently placed near the telephone. There may, at first, be a nagging doubt as to whether you will double-book someone; it will soon pass, and shouldn't happen if you are wary and double-check. Fortnightly bookings are the ones to watch for — hence the need for a wall chart. Ask for a small deposit whatever the period involved. As regards weekends, it occasionally happens — especially if the weather takes a turn for the worst — that people decide not to bother, and you are left holding a room (and in a dilemma as to how long to save it). Having refused other would-be guests a room because you *think* you are full, and then finding yourself in a situation where the erring party fails to arrive, is annoying to say the least. Although there will be exceptions, communication is perhaps the keyword. Try and tie up approximately what time your guests will be arriving and politely request a deposit, then, should they not send it nor arrive within two hours of the approximate arrival time, it would be wise simply to let their rooms, if you are otherwise full. It is bad business practice not to do so; you must have some sort of deadline and ruling. No deposit, no booking. It would be impossible to run your hotel any other way.

Mention was made above of *pencilling* tentative enquiries in your reservation book. This may sound trifling, but when people change their minds as to dates, cancel altogether, decide they would like a shower room instead, or, where perhaps two ladies are involved: 'We're just phoning to ask if another, larger room is available, with an extra bed; our Aunt Ethel wants to join us...' you can imagine what an unholy mess a booking book can get into. It is a simple enough matter to ink in pencilled details when you receive confirmation in writing *and* a deposit (always noting the amount of the deposit against the booking). There will be the odd exception where genuine illness occurs after a deposit has been received and everything is neatly inscribed in ink, but you don't expect to win every round. The neater your book, the easier your task will be when referring to it for accounting purposes.

Postal bookings

Here, time really is of the essence, and the quicker you can get a reply to a tentative enquiry or booking into the post, the better. Postal bookings usually necessitate two letters from both parties; the initial request for details from the interested party, your reply; their deposit and your confirmation. Again, careful note of all pertinent details should be made in the booking book, the appropriate correspondence kept stapled or clipped in for easy reference when needed, and only removed when the guest has settled the bill and departed. Regrettably, some people are a little vague when it comes to writing for details and may state a date which doesn't tally with the day it should. Even when you feel sure that a booking is from Saturday to Saturday and the person mentions arriving on Friday's date, it is best to check. Some enquirers enclose a stamped, self-addressed envelope and some don't, and the same goes for hoteliers; it depends what train of thought you follow — postage is expensive but can bring in more business.

Printing needs

Brochures and postcards bearing a likeness or photograph of your hotel are your ambassadors, going out to greet members of the public for the most part unaware of your existence, so the fairer the image the better. Such printed matter should be of the best quality you can afford, without going over the top, and original in design where possible. The design is most important, the aim being to catch the eye. When inheriting a mass of boring printed parapher-nalia, study it and see what you can come up with to strengthen the image and give it more appeal. It could be a motif tying in with the name of your hotel, road, area, or a specific landmark etc. Give the matter thought, as it will pay off.

In the main, you will need either a reasonably sized tariff post-card or brochure, or both, letterheads and invoices, and can top up with additional promotional cards or posters at a later date.

Settling customers' bills

The whole question of settling bills can be ticklish or even delicate at first, especially if you are new to the business. To make life easier (and enable you to sleep more soundly in your bed) make a few rules and stick to them. Decide on a certain procedure (clearly printed on a suitable card and displayed in a prominent position in the reception area or near your tariff-board) such as, 'Please present cheques for payment four days before departure to allow time for clearance' or something of the sort — obviously applying to weekly or fortnightly holiday-makers — and see that guests comply with your wishes. The odd cheque does bounce, so it is as well not to take chances. Naturally, when guests are staying for a short period only and wish to pay by cheque, they are required to produce a cheque guarantee card.

Some members of the public seem to feel the urgent need to settle up as soon as they are over the threshold: 'We'll know what we have left to spend then' is a popular comment. On the other hand, unless you strictly adhere to your ruling, you will meet a few awkward guests who seem loath to part with their money or cheques until after they have digested the last crumb of their departure breakfast toast and marmalade. Thankfully, the major-ity seem only too happy to pay as you suggest.

These days, many hotels, particularly the larger ones, insist that bills are settled when guests book in, so you should not feel embarrassed when asking for payment. This applies more to pass-ing trade where there is no correspondence or proved address for, regrettably, there are undesirable characters roaming the country looking for an 'easy' proprietor and free bed and breakfast.

The usual procedure is for an invoice, bearing the name, address and details of length of stay and any extras involved, to be handed to the guest; it is receipted when payment is made. A copy is always kept for accounting purposes (either on a metal spike for safe-keeping, or stapled with other copy invoices for the appropriate period in the booking book at the end of each week).

Pets

While separate holidays for pets and owners are popular, and the kennel business seems to be booming, there are still many dog owners who take their pets away with them. Whether you take in animals or not is purely a matter of personal preference, and therefore attitudes differ from hotel to hotel. However, even if you are fond of dogs, when running a small business with little garden space, housing more than one animal can be a problem. Animal-loving proprietors of slightly larger guest houses or hotels based in the country have the obvious advantage of more space inside and out.

Despite the fact that the English are, by and large, a dog-loving nation, it is worth bearing in mind that, even though most caring dog owners can and do control their pets, there are the canine 'yappers' to take into account. It is advisable, when booking in people with dogs, to have their assurance of the animal's good behaviour, and to enforce a ruling that pets are not allowed in the dining-room.

When advertising, time and misunderstanding are saved if you state 'No pets' or 'Pets welcome', whatever your stand. Whether a charge is made for housing dogs is, of course, dependent on any outgoings incurred (most owners meet their own pet's needs, fresh water often being the only requirement as far as the hotelier is concerned).

Laundry

While you may have your own ideas or leanings as to just what proportion of the laundering is carried out on hotel premises (perhaps dictated by facilities, or lack of them, size of hotel — hence volume of business, and time element), hotels in the main, especially when working at full capacity, tend to send out the bulk of their laundry for professional attention. Competition between laundries — and the consequent differences in charges — is keen, more particularly when there is a high density of hotels in an area creating a density of attendant laundry business. This can work in the hotelier's favour and you can choose a firm of launderers in the knowledge that, where competition is keen, the service (if the company is worth its salt) will be a good one. Again, only time and trial will tell.

Depending on your existing store of linen — some vendors leave more ample provision than others — two main procedures can be followed:

1. Make a few enquiries; peruse prices of two or three laundries; select a suitable company to call and collect soiled linen which will then be duly laundered and returned on specific days.
2. Hire linen (where prices compare favourably with normal laundry service). This is a procedure whereby a company's linen is loaned to the hotelier — an initial fee being chargeable, which is returned at cessation of service. Soiled linen is then collected, laundered and returned in the same manner as a straightforward laundry service.

Where compatibly priced (areas vary here) the hire scheme is worth considering. Not only are you preserving your own store of linen (maybe choosing to dovetail the use of your own stock when business is exceptionally brisk or quiet, especially by using coloured drip-dry linen for home laundering), but your own stock gains an extended life expectancy, and is readily available in an emergency.

It is worth noting that where inherited linen is in a bad condition, or meagre, the hiring procedure need only be a temporary measure while building up a stock.

In the winter months, it may be decided to more or less dispense with hiring for, as business slackens, home laundering is not such a problem (again, provided there are adequate drying facilities in bad weather). Much depends on the condition and quantity of linen left by the vendor, size of hotel, and staff or lack of them.

Whatever laundry arrangements are decided upon, ample linen store cupboards or chests are required. Whereas in larger establishments, linen maids or housekeepers are responsible for the condition, flow and repair of linen, and for the general order of storage areas, the poor old head-cook and bottle-washer will have to take this task in her stride. In a smaller business, the sheer volume of linen is not as daunting as that which faces proprietors of larger hotels. Of course, it is true that in larger hotels staff ease the owner's problems.

Check that all linen storage areas and cupboards are clean and dry, and where linen is not in use over long periods, cover it to keep it clean.

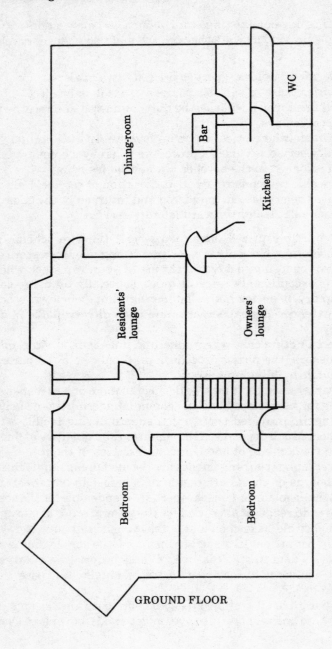

GROUND FLOOR

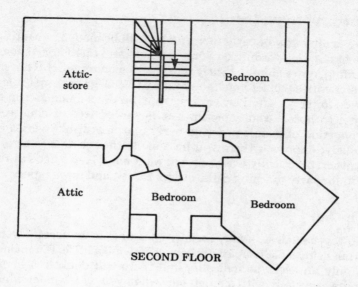

SECOND FLOOR

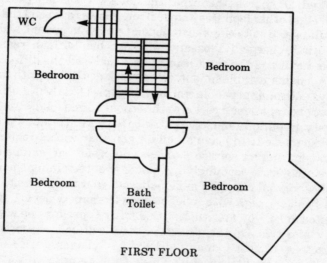

FIRST FLOOR

Example of simple plan of hotel and bar site.
Plans need not necessarily be drawn up by an architect
(which could prove expensive), but they do need to be
drawn to scale.

SCALE 1,100 APPROX

Early morning tea

The availability of early morning tea will be made known to your
guests by the wording on your brochure and tariff-board, usually
reading, quite simply: 'Early morning tea on request'. Those who
prefer coffee will let you know. An extra charge per cup is usually
made for serving either, varying from 5p to as much as 15p from
hotel to hotel. And sometimes it is served free of charge. The
proportion of people ordering early morning drinks varies enormously; one week there will be none (although this is rare) and
another, practically everyone will want one. Keep a book at reception for early morning calls, orders for tea and newspapers.

The bar

However modest, a bar, socially speaking, is an asset. Even one
drink helps most people to relax and unwind a little. Financially, it
is only an asset periodically, and there will doubtless be times
(more especially with a small bar) when you will wonder why you
bothered. Of course, the larger the hotel and the more attractive
the bar and other facilities (dance floor, games room etc) the higher
the takings. But takings also depend on management's attitude
and prices charged! Pleasant, efficient bar staff, a reasonable
drinks tariff and the right atmosphere make all the difference.

In a smaller establishment, to be stuck at the bar with two (not
always enthralling) people who buy a couple of 'halves' and share a
packet of crisps over a period of three hours, is no joke — unless you
are very gregarious and have patience to spare. The answer to such
a predicament is to leave a bell on your bar with a request that
customers ring for service — unless you prefer bar leaning that is.
There are guests seemingly incapable of entertaining themselves
at all, who would happily monopolise *all* your time. Unlike a shop,
where you can sigh with relief as such customers depart after ten
minutes or so, you are stuck with similar types for one week, and
sometimes two. On the plus side, there will be an assortment of
characters to meet — many a delight to converse with — which
leads to another little problem; if you don't enforce a 'last orders'
time, you could be stuck at the bar until the small hours of the
morning. However charming your guests and interesting the conversation, there are chores to attend to before hitting the sack, and
you can't make up for it in the mornings either. If you over-indulge
people with your precious time and burn the candle consistently at
both ends, you will end up feeling — and looking — like a zombie. It
is sometimes a little difficult to get the balance just right.

One enjoyable aspect of having a licence is being able to serve wine and liqueurs at dinner. You are, after all, serving drinks to make a profit. Forecasting is difficult. One week's takings will rarely match the next. You may have reason to feel optimistic when a party of six arrive, ask to share a table and proceed to order doubles of everything before the first course arrives. It could be the pattern for the week, you muse in the kitchen (rubbing your hands). However, when a different sextet sit down to dine the following week, don't count your chickens; it could be a case of two teetotallers, two 'I'll av arf's' and a couple of fruit juice addicts.

Unless you have a larger hotel and bar, your drinks profit margin won't always be as high as you would like, especially in a family hotel where, some weeks, children and older people make up over half of your intake. The exceptional periods should be Easter and Christmas (especially) and any weeks you house rugby clubs (lock up your daughters and batten down the hatches), bowling clubs etc. At the end of such weeks (unless you have bar staff) expect to feel in need of a blood transfusion.

The licence
If the hotel you take on has an existing drinks licence, it is usually a simple matter of transferring it to the new owner. Your solicitor will arrange for you to appear briefly in court and, unless you are particularly undesirable, or there are extenuating circumstances, there should be no problems.

The licence will enable you to sell drinks and tobacco. It is an offence to sell alcohol to or for the consumption of children under 18 years old; tobacco in any form is embargoed until the age of 16.

If, on the other hand, there is no existing licence to serve alcohol, and no bar as such, there are procedures to be followed to obtain a residential licence. Plans of your premises will need to be drawn up and submitted in triplicate (through your solicitor): one of the hotel and adjacent streets and area, and one of the hotel itself, indicating where you intend installing the bar. In compliance with the Licensing Act 1964, an official 'Notice of Application' should be displayed by you for a period of not less than seven days — prior to the day of the sessions — in a place where it can conveniently be read by the public on or near the premises to be licensed. During this period, no fewer than three magistrates and/or suitably responsible persons will require to see a copy of your plans, view the exact site of the proposed bar, and ask one or two relevant questions. After the hearing and the granting of the residential licence, a member of the police force (Crime Prevention Officer) will call on you with suggestions as to locking entrances and exits, actual bar door/shutter etc, and you are required to comply with such suggestions and inform the police that you have done so.

The court hearing itself can take anything from 20 minutes to two hours and the procedure is simple enough. (Put by around £250 for the solicitor's fees.)

Setting up the bar

Setting up even a modest bar can be an expensive business, quite apart from the building of the bar itself. There are the drinks, optics and other measures, ice buckets etc. If you can build up your stock gradually, it will obviously be less of a shock to your monetary system. Always have a plentiful supply of ice (even well-stocked bars are guilty of running out too soon). If you intend serving drinks yourself (or on a rota system with one or two others) see that at least one of you is initiated into the mysteries of the bar. Brush up on your knowledge of what ingredients go into the making of what drinks. Drink fads and fancies are forever changing. A lot depends on how much of a feature you wish to make of your bar, what time you have to spare, what assistance is available, and the actual drink capacity of the number of guests staying. It can be as modestly or as well stocked a bar as you care to make it. Whatever you decide upon, don't forget important trimmings like cherries, lemon slices etc, and stock a small supply of assorted nuts and crisps; a large stock will not keep fresh when the volume of business is small.

For a smaller business, the purchase of a quantity of canned or bottled beer would be more desirable than barrelled. While the heavier demands of the summer season would, of course, necessitate keeping larger stocks, the purchase of barrelled beer should be approached with caution because of its shorter store life.

Empties

When dealing with breweries and ordering barrels and bottles of beer on a regular basis, an arrangement is made whereby empties are collected by the respective brewery. Beer cans or bottles bought from supermarkets or off licences can be disposed of in paladins when empty although larger quantities of bottles should be deposited in a bottle-bank if at all possible.

Where a bar is already installed, the vendor should leave the purchaser a fair supply of glassware; just how much will often depend on the price, type and size of hotel, and the size of the bar itself. Here again, check the inventory early on. If a feature has been made of the bar, the proprietor will doubtless be proud of it, in which case you can safely assume that there will be an ample supply of traditionally shaped and appropriate glassware, namely:

Beer glasses. 12 fluid ounces for bottled beer; pint and half pint for draught beer. Draught beer and cider may only be sold in quantities of one-third or one-half pint or in multiples of a half pint. Plain and decorated glass mugs or tankards for beer (sometimes supplied through breweries).

Wine and spirit glasses. Stemmed glasses, Paris goblets for example, 5, 6-2/3 and 8 fl oz; there is no legal requirement as to size, but a code of practice is in preparation and will probably allow a choice of two sizes for wine, separated by 2 fl oz or 50 ml. Spirits must be sold in quantities or multiples of one-fourth, one-fifth or one-sixth of a gill. A variety of bottle optics and stainless steel or silver measures can be purchased from catering shops.

Liqueur glasses are small stemmed glasses. One-third of a gill is the legal measure, or multiples of it.

Port and sherry glasses are like wine glasses but smaller, usually around 2½ fl oz capacity.

Brandy glasses are usually 5½ fl oz; the rim has a smaller diameter than the girth of the bowl, to retain the aroma.

Champagne glasses. Tulip-shape is the trade preference, but the saucer-shape is still popularly used.

The dining-room

Tables
The laying of the dining-room table can be an art form in itself. Silver service, whereby a waiter or waitress serves a customer from a silver platter or tureen, using silver cutlery, is still called for and popular in the larger or more exclusive hotels and in high class restaurants, but is rarely used in more modest hotels and guest houses. Durable, easy-care place mats are an advantage and pleasing where colour-matched and, of course, some table decoration, however simple.

Cutlery
Most hoteliers accept stainless steel cutlery as commonplace these days and, although, quite naturally, silver is still widely used in the more exclusive hotels, the use of stainless steel is becoming

more widespread. Beautifully kept silver is undoubtedly lovely, graces a well thought-out table and adds class to the whole scene; sadly, it is also expensive and more troublesome to care for. Good quality stainless steel is reasonably priced in comparison, looks good and is simplicity itself to look after. Bone-handled cutlery was once very fashionable — quickly followed by plastic and nylon facsimiles, but all are liable to discoloration and are therefore not a good idea. Well-equipped hotels often boast adequate matching cutlery. When replacing cutlery, confirm that it is comfortable to hold and well-balanced, bottom-heavy cutlery being an embarrassment and a nuisance to both staff and guests.

Glassware

Water jugs and tumblers are usually in evidence for use in the dining-room, and small glasses for serving fruit juice. You will also require an ample supply of dessert dishes, both large and small, banana split dishes, and a variety of serving bowls and preparing bowls. List what is available when you are taking over a hotel for future reference.

Condiment sets

These can be pottery, glass, silver or stainless steel. Whatever their design and material, check that they are easily recognisable and easy to clean. Cruet sets that match crockery are popular and look attractive in a homely setting; silver condiment sets are perhaps best left for special days (again because of cleaning).

Marmalade/jam pots, butter dishes or pre-packaged portions

Purely for convenience's sake, many hotels favour pre-packaged portions of butter, marmalade, jam, sauce, mayonnaise and so on. Personally I believe that pre-packaged everything smacks of a cafe and is to be avoided; individual butter pats and perhaps mayonnaise and salad cream portions are a good idea — although care should always be taken that they are kept cool. Preference for mayonnaise or salad cream varies enormously, and doling out portions in dishes for every table is not only time-consuming but wasteful (as with mustard, much is thrown away). Pots containing marmalade, jam and honey are not such a problem but, here too, keep them in a cool place where possible and only half-fill containers so that consumption of the contents is quicker, thereby ensuring that the guest is served with produce as fresh as possible.

Service trays, ashtrays and toast racks

Round trays are popular when serving drinks at tables or in the bar; check that surfaces are suitable to prevent glasses sliding. The trays that you are left may not be suitable or adequate, and you will need trays that are 'silent', durable and strong, but light in weight and of varying sizes. Trays for morning teas should be smaller than those used for transporting crockery to and from the dining-room.

Sturdy ashtrays should be used for obvious reasons; check that the rim prevents cigarettes and cigars from falling on to cloths or cushions and becoming fire risks, and that they hold the ash in a draught.

Stainless steel toast racks (large and small) are the most convenient for reasons of weight, durability and ease of cleaning.

Tea and coffee pots and water jugs

Stainless steel teapots, coffee pots and hot water jugs are prevalent in many hotels. The breakages to chinaware are avoided, hence saving expense. However, do check that hinges are in good working order. Nevertheless, it is said that a china teapot produces a better cup of tea, and china can look most attractive. Should you decide on china, ensure that it is more durable than that used in private households; it will certainly need to stand up to greater tests of strength! Most catering crockery is thicker than household china for this very reason. Tannin stains build up if not checked, so regular cleaning is essential.

Tureens or vegetable dishes

Many proprietors of smaller guest houses and hotels serve meals already plated, possibly assuming that the use of tureens is the prerogative of grander hotels. This is rather a pity as there are a few reasons why their use is desirable:

1. Individuals can help themselves to the quantity and type of vegetable which they prefer. Pre-plated meals, piled high with too many potatoes or a disliked vegetable, are offputting and to be avoided.
2. The use of tureens saves the embarrassment felt when a guest has to eat around a particular vegetable they dislike (they may remember to tell you they don't eat pork or fish but rarely itemise other dislikes).

Tureens and vegetable dishes are made from various materials, eg, china, pottery, Pyrex, stainless steel and silver. Silver tureens do look rather splendid but are expensive and need care and time, whereas stainless steel is easy to clean and care for, and there is the added bonus of durability.

Chapter 8
Staffing

Even when selecting staff on a small scale, it is natural to want the best available; a really capable part-timer can prove just as invaluable as a full-time employee, especially on a Saturday (the usual change-over day).

Obviously, a small hotelier in need of just one part-time assistant — perhaps to help with the domestic work — has less of a problem than the proprietor of a larger establishment who needs to employ several full-time people, as well as a few on a part-time basis. Nevertheless, those few working hours needed are still vital to the smooth running of a small hotel, and however minor their role, potential staff still need to be interviewed and chosen. After an interview, prospective employers will at least have some idea of what the applicant is capable of. Whether such capabilities will be adequate and satisfactory when practically applied, only time will tell.

Usually, there is no shortage of applicants for part-time employment; hoteliers receive many phone calls, letters and personal introductions from people seeking hotel work (more especially in the height of the season when students are on holiday and seek temporary employment). If, perhaps for reasons of location, hotel staff *are* difficult to come by, you may need to advertise in your local paper, seek the services of an employment agency or the help of local Employment Department offices.

When making a final decision as to the right person for the job, do make working arrangements, times, wages, and any other conditions involved, as clear as possible. It is worth making a list of the jobs you want your staff to do. This list can form the basis of an advertisement and, when interviewing, you can use it as a checklist for each applicant.

Engagement

The formalities that attend an interview where the applicant needs some specific expertise and the requirements are more complicated can usually be dispensed with when interviewing part-time staff required to perform menial tasks. Such staff will still need common sense, honesty, enthusiasm and an ability to work unsupervised where necessary, but obviously the interview would be shorter and (although it should still be businesslike) more informal. Confirm that all conditions are understood.

Employees who work more than 16 hours a week for you will need a contract of employment. The Department of Employment issues a leaflet which covers the subject in detail, 'Written statement of main terms and conditions of employment', and this is available from Social Security Offices and Employment Offices. The contract can be quite simple and should state the job title, the rate of pay and how frequently it is paid, working hours, holidays and holiday pay, sick pay provision, pension provision, the notice required by both parties, disciplinary rules and grievance procedure.

If your staff earn more than the £43.00 a week lower limit for the payment of tax and National Insurance contributions, you will be responsible for the deductions from their wages. Your local tax office will provide tax tables and a tax deduction card for each employee. You will need to produce an itemised pay statement for each employee on pay day, showing gross and net wages, deductions and any overtime. At the end of the tax year, you should provide each employee with a summary of payments and deductions for the past year (or that part of the year worked) on form P60; a complementary summary, on form P35, is sent to the Inland Revenue. When employees leave, they will each require from you a completed form P45.

National Insurance contributions are deducted from pay, along with PAYE, and information is obtainable from Social Security Offices in leaflets NP15 'Employer's Guide to National Insurance Contributions' and NI 208 'National Insurance Contribution Rates'.

Dismissal

An employer must give an employee at least one week's notice if the employee has worked continuously for a period of between one month and two years, two weeks' notice thereafter and an additional week for each year of continuous employment up to 12 years' continuous service. This does not apply to part-time employees who work less than 16 hours a week unless they have worked for the same employer for at least eight hours a week for at least five years, continuously.

However few hours your assistant works, your need will be for someone reliable, honest and efficient. If such a person is unable to maintain reasonable, simple and basic standards, it would be foolish to keep him/her in your employ. You can ill-afford any slipping of standards in the running of your hotel. In some circumstances, you may find the dismissal of staff a painful process. If you are half-hearted about dismissing an assistant, it would be worth having a talk in the first instance: he/she may improve. If not, dismissal is the only remedy.

Supervision

The larger the hotel, the more work there is involved in supervising staff and planning the work-load. Delegation is a much simpler matter when running a small hotel. The ideal situation exists when an assistant is found to be totally reliable and can be left unsupervised; much valuable time can be lost checking up that work is carried out satisfactorily. Many female proprietors, acting as housekeepers, and used to doing their own housework, work alongside their assistants, knowing their 'treasures' can be left at any given moment to carry on. This is particularly comforting at the weekend. Saturday — the usual change-over day — can be frantically busy and usually is in the summer season. Some guests arrive before they are expected; others travel on overnight coaches and arrive for breakfast. The day is peppered with departures and arrivals. Occasionally, when guests are sluggish in departing, new arrivals have to be fed and watered. Fortunately, for all those guests arriving too early, there are more who arrive late, sandwiching those who are punctual to the half-hour. This all emphasises the need for a good, reliable chambermaid.

Salaries

When employing a person on a part-time basis, especially only for a few hours at the weekend, an hourly rate is agreed upon, and payment usually made in cash for hours worked. It really is as simple as that. Provided one keeps within the earnings ceiling specified by the income tax authorities — at present £43 per week — the arrangement should work to everyone's advantage. Should you decide to employ full-time or more staff, or perhaps increase the earning capacity of your assistant, further information can be obtained from your local Employment or Inland Revenue Office (see page 38) or your accountant may be asked for advice.

Legal requirements

It would be advisable to check the Health and Safety at Work Act 1974 with your local Health and Safety Executive Office. The available free literature would tell you what is relevant to your business, especially on the prevention and reporting of accidents.

The Equal Pay Act, Sex Discrimination Act and the Race Relations Act all need to be taken into account when advertising for or engaging staff. Newspaper advertising departments will usually tell you if your advertisement needs amendment.

Chapter 9
Buying

It is imperative to the smooth-running of your hotel that the whole business of buying supplies, both perishable and otherwise, is carefully organised. You will need to find one, two and maybe three reliable outlets. There are five main sources to consider:

1. Cash and carry outlets
2. Supermarkets
3. Door-to-door delivery service
4. Freezer centres
5. Smaller stores and shops

Cash and carry outlets

Unless you have bought a high proportion of your predecessor's perishable and unperishable stock, you will need to call on a cash and carry outlet (especially for catering-size products) to refill food cupboards, fridges and freezers etc, and to ensure that you carry an ample supply of toiletries, washing powder, disinfectant and other unperishable items. There is sometimes more than one cash and carry business in the vicinity of a large town; in such cases, competition — and therefore price-cutting — will be keener. This is, of course, an ideal situation from the purchaser's point of view. Word soon gets round when one outlet is superior, better stocked and more given to 'special offers' than another. Also, there is no shortage of advertising material from such places, which sets out — usually in bold colour — just what those special offers are.

When taking over a hotel in the late autumn, winter or early spring (particularly when there is no intention of operating immediately), it is worth investigating such places for yourself while there is time to spare. Bear in mind that prices have a habit of spiralling upwards as the high season approaches, so it is to your advantage to stock up in advance where feasible. Cash and carry businesses are doubtless aware of the unavailability of large, catering-sized items elsewhere, and sometimes the saving involved is disappointingly small. Nevertheless, such places do fulfil a need, particularly in respect of dried, tinned and perishable goods. Round about March (with Easter trade on the horizon) you could start your own paper-chase with the various leaflets, brochures and advertising paraphernalia received. Hesitate before throwing it *all* in the bin and have a browse through — saving a pound here and a pound there is what it is about.

An easy error to make when first shopping at a cash and carry is temporarily to forget (or not realise) that VAT has to be added to the listed cost of purchases, where applicable, at the cash desk. When registered for VAT you would, of course, be reimbursed after a period of time (naturally, having first made a VAT payment).

Supermarkets

It is no secret that supermarkets in general are becoming more competitive, widening their choice of products, both perishable and otherwise, and are convenient places in which to shop. Special offers abound and, where there are two or more supermarkets in competition, you will be hard put to keep up with it all. However, it really is worth keeping your eyes open and, after a trial period, you will no doubt find a system of shopping to fit in with your routine.

Door-to-door delivery service

Firms operating such a service are as keen and competitive as the High Street supermarkets and, particularly for the caterer/ hotelier, fulfil an urgent need, more so when the house is full and you are trying to do three things at once! Most frozen foods offered by such firms are of a high standard (their noses would soon be out of joint otherwise) and, like sampling the wares of the cash and carry outlet and the supermarkets, you would do well to have a small, trial order delivered to your door. It is then only a matter of time before you decide which firm has the edge regarding quality, price and delivery.

Freezer centres

As an alternative to the delivery service (or as well as) freezer centres are worthy of attention. Along with all the other food outlets, they offer weekly cut-price products for your consideration. Such centres are sprouting up like daffodils in spring, so you should be able to locate one, unless you have chosen an isolated spot for your hotel.

Smaller stores and shops

Generally speaking, smaller stores and shops are more expensive — they obviously have to be to compete with their larger, richer brothers. But here too, occasionally, special offers are made which may be worth investigating. Much depends on the season and time available. Even when running a business efficiently, human error has to be taken into account — the odd item does get overlooked (milk is a good example, especially in off-peak periods). It is at such times that you will bless the little shop around the corner.

Shopping routine

Once you have all the different sources taped and you become more familiar with the routine imposed by running a guest house or hotel, a suitable method of shopping for your needs will present itself, eg:

1. Perhaps have your freezer well or partially filled by the delivery company (the only time involved will be the putting-away and noting of new stock on your list). Here you save on petrol *and* time.
2. Go along to the cash and carry once a month to top up (the frequency of shopping trips and the time spent on them can be tailored as necessary). There are those who prefer to buy enormous quantities of everything, thereby saving time and petrol, and those who think it shrewd to keep a watch on fluctuating prices. It is probably a case of swings and roundabouts.
3. Use freezer centres to complement other suppliers where necessary.
4. Visit supermarkets weekly for items which have been tried, tested and found good value. Such trips can couple up with a visit to the freezer centre, again saving some valuable time at least.

There are several alternatives for obtaining items such as eggs and other fresh produce (fruit and vegetables, and meat).

The milkman
More particularly in high hotel-density areas, milkmen carry a supply of different products (orders are given in advance, of course) including eggs, butter, fats, creams, yoghurt, and sometimes bread and cakes.

The greengrocer
It is a boon to find a reliable greengrocer who delivers produce of a high standard at a realistic price.

The egg-man
Many farms run a delivery service and, when hotels are thick on the ground, competition, therefore price-cutting, is keener.

The butcher
Although you can, of course, buy your meat at the cash and carry outlet, the freezer centre or the supermarket — and don't forget the High Street butcher — there are several mobile butchers around and the quality, price and general standard of their service should be looked into.

Miscellaneous

Watch out for salesmen plying their trade at your door; there will be quite a few — some good, some bad. However, many bargains can be bought in such items as towels, carpets, miscellaneous household goods, plants and table decorations. One lesson learned early on was being taken in by 'fantastic saving bargains' claims, in particular where prices quoted did not include VAT. The salesman assured me his firm's products were 'cheaper than any cash and carry or supermarket you care to name...' They were — *before* VAT. I duly complained and the firm in question graciously reduced the price (which was still slightly above that of the price charged at the local supermarket). You have been warned.

Chapter 10

Food and Drink

It is a fair assumption that, along with the weather, food ranks high on the list for complete holiday enjoyment, and the serving of good food becomes even more prominent when the weather proves a disappointment; returning from a soggy day in the great outdoors to find an indifferent meal waiting can be the last straw.

There are countless books on the market covering anything from the humble potato to the most extravagantly dressed fresh salmon. Whether it is your intention to take your guests on a culinary journey around the world with such dishes as Jou Yuan Ts'a Hui (Meatballs Chop Suey) or Chicken Tikka (Spicy Chicken Kebabs) or stay on familiar terra firma with traditional English dishes, do see that you do your absolute best by whatever you serve. It is certainly more commendable (and probably more digestible) to offer a simple dish you excel at rather than an extravagant one you are unsure of. Nevertheless, there are many simple dishes with names evocative of faraway places with which to titillate your guests' palates occasionally.

However, if your hotel has a strong traditional flavour, you would do well to concentrate on good home cooking, or offer dishes indigenous to your own or the adjoining county. All this assumes that you will be doing either the lion's share of the cooking, or splitting the duties with a partner. Even where a chef is involved, you will need to cooperate and discuss menus, and take a lively, active interest in the food being served to your guests if you wish your hotel to be a success.

Familiar dishes are preferred

One slight drawback to running a mainly 'family/passing-trade' type of hotel, is the reluctance of the average Mr and Mrs to try anything other than 'Good, plain cooking, please.' There is absolutely nothing wrong with good English dishes but the English in general have long been unadventurous in their eating habits. This trait seems to belong mainly to the over fifty-fives and, notably, the male sex. However, tastes are gradually changing, cheaper foreign travel and cheap exotic imports having enabled many to sample and enjoy dishes once known only to the rich. For some odd reason (old habits die hard) many still scorn foreign, or foreign-sounding foods, or unusual dishes, and stick to fish and chips, pie and mash, steak-and-kidney pie, the popular roasts, chicken and other poultry (served plain, undisguised and unadorned), plus two or three basic vegetables. All of these are excellent when cooked with care and served with imagination, but it is refreshing occasionally when people are a little daring in their tastes.

During a trial period of one year, my husband and I noted that most guests (again in the fifty and upwards age group, and more particularly among the men) cocked a snook at corn-on-the cob, courgettes, ratatouille — far too French-sounding — anything remotely oriental or 'foreign', too many sauces, rice dishes, spaghetti and other pasta dishes. This observation was borne out by several other hotel and guest house proprietors. It seems that many prefer that with which they are more familiar.

Occasionally, it works out that guests are split into two, quite separate age groups (perhaps parties of people holidaying together), thus enabling you to vary the menu. The younger age group could welcome anything from moussaka to quarter-pound hamburgers (the young, too, can be conservative in their tastes), while the older group may choose to stick to their roasts. Nevertheless, if a hotel is run by a small staff there is a limit to the time that can be spent at the cooker! There is a lot to be said, in the busy summer season especially, for keeping to a simple, set menu. From the costing point of view it is more economical to serve traditional fare, with perhaps some slight variation occasionally. Less familiar vegetables and ingredients, and some of the more exotic fruits, can be a drain on your resources when your tariff has been set too low to accommodate such expensive items. One has, after all, to budget in advance and it is difficult to deviate too much without feeling the pinch. Quite apart from a financial viewpoint, it is frustrating to splash out on something just a little bit special or unusual only to have it returned when the tureens are cleared. Get to know your main market and cater for it — it will be more rewarding in the long run, and leave those special dishes you may have in mind for any gourmet weekends later on in the year.

Balancing the food and courses, both from a desirable and financial angle, is a case of swings and roundabouts. It is obviously more profitable to serve a slightly expensive hors-d'oeuvre one day, followed by a modestly priced main course and sweet, and alternate the courses cost-wise throughout the week (such as most housewives have to on a much smaller scale). Your profit margin will depend on what's in season and the price, what you have wisely frozen when at its cheapest, how ingenious you are, and what bargains you have been lucky enough to find. Anyone who has attended a catering course knows only too well about such juggling and management problems. After some experimenting and experience, however, even the novice can triumph if diligent and caring.

Should you wish to appeal to more adventurous palates, gourmet weekends would present a challenge, provide catering variety, and a welcome source of income when the summer rush is over. Of course, your tariff will have to be in step.

Set menus

Unless offering an à la carte table, for practical reasons, you will probably find it more convenient and economical to keep to a set menu for a week at a time. However, two weeks of repetitious food is a bit much on holiday for the fortnightly guests, unless it is their choice, of course. Even if you choose to have a chicken dish on the menu each week, there are numerous ways of serving it and the same applies to other meats and fish dishes.

Depending on whether you plan running a very homely, easy-going guest house or hotel with maximum personal participation, or one where more staff are employed (with you behind the scenes) menus can be professionally printed, typed or simply conveyed by word of mouth. Either way, it is convenient if the evening's menu is discussed immediately after breakfast. From the guest's point of view, there is nothing more embarrassing than having a plate bearing something he dislikes, plonked down in a 'take it or leave it' manner. There are bound to be people who dislike fish, pork, or whatever; and with such ample warning, there is more than enough time to prepare an alternative. Some of the smaller guest houses and hotels do not offer any alternative at all, which seems very short-sighted on their part.

Much care should be given to planning and balancing your menus, quite apart from the costing of them. For instance, a meal consisting of soup and a bread roll, steak-and-kidney pie, vegetables and potatoes, followed by sultana pudding and custard, could cost the same to provide as chilled grapefruit, the same main course, finishing off with a sorbet or fruit jelly and cream. On a hot day, the majority would, most likely, prefer the latter. This may seem elementary to the experienced hotelier or chef but, to the novice, it is an easy error to offer the heavier menu. By a process of trial and error, my husband and I found that six of the all-time favourites, with the average summertime guest, were the following:

Tomato, or other Soup/Fruit Juice
(Roll and Butter)

Fried Plaice/Cod with Lemon
(around half declined Tartare Sauce)
Sauté Potatoes/French Fried Potatoes and Peas

Apple Pie and Cream/Ice Cream

★

Fresh Grapefruit/Fruit Juice

Steak-and-Kidney Pie
Boiled or Creamed Potatoes
Mixed Vegetables/Spring Greens/Carrots

Crème Caramel/Cheese and Biscuits

★

Pâté/Fruit Juice
(the former preferred by a younger age group)

Boiled Bacon/Baked Ham
with Pineapple/Pease Pudding
Runner Beans/Butter Beans/Carrots
Boiled or Creamed Potatoes

Banana Split/Ice Cream Gateau/
Baked Alaska/Peach Melba

★

Fresh Melon/Grapefruit

Roast Chicken
Roast Potatoes
Brussels Sprouts/Cauliflower/Peas
(around half declined Sauce)

Gateau/Fresh Fruit Salad

★

Fish Starter/Egg Mayonnaise
(around half declined the latter)

Roast Pork and Apple Sauce
(very few older people like Sweet and Sour Sauce)
Dunkirk Potatoes
Buttered Carrots/Parsnips/Peas

Trifle/Fresh Fruit Salad

★

Soup (especially Oxtail, Minestrone
and thicker soups)
(Roll and Butter)

Ham/Cheese/Egg/Fish Salad with
New Potatoes/Jacket Potatoes

Date/Sultana/Banana/Bread-and-Butter Pudding
served with Cream or Custard

As you see, quite modest fare is popular with the majority. Beef, lamb, turkey and braising steak are also equally in demand, roast meat perhaps being a firmer favourite. Nothing too difficult for you or your chef there.

A few other random observations revealed that, in the main, quiches and vol au vents were preferred by younger people; cheese and biscuits are chosen with more frequency by the men than the ladies; many (even quite elderly) ladies will leave a portion of the main meal but not a scrap of their gateau, or other desserts. Heavy drinkers are poor eaters! Two other points worth a mention: *always* have a bowl of fresh fruit to offer and, of course, a cheese board.

Ready-prepared food

Some hoteliers rely more heavily on frozen, pre-cooked, or uncooked pies, sweet and savoury etc, than others. There is absolutely nothing wrong with the *best* of these, particularly when demands are heavy on your time. There is no point in being a martyr (and a rather tired one at that). If you insist on making every dish yourself, you will only succeed in wearing yourself to a frazzle. I refer, of course, to the busy summer season. If you enjoy cooking or contributing to some of the dishes to emerge from your kitchen, you can do so with less pressure once the autumn leaves start to fall. This is the time to prepare for Christmas, and to cook stand-by dishes for storing in your freezer. In the meantime, don't despise frozen pastry; it is an excellent aid to the busy cook.

Breakfast

There is occasionally a rigid attitude as to what breakfast should consist of. It can be a drag to cook porridge, kippers and a selection of fried food but, when catering for people's tastes (and that, after all, is what hotelkeeping is about) it has to be accepted that there will be mornings when more than the eternal fried breakfast is required. There are places where either cornflakes or fruit juice is served *every* morning; with such a variety of cereals on the market, surely this is unimaginative thinking. Believing themselves to be very shrewd, the hoteliers who offer only cornflakes or the dilutable fruit juice are fooling no one but themselves. The same type of hotelier is sometimes guilty of serving meat so thin one can read the paper through it; offering meagre helpings; buying the cheapest cuts of meat; providing inadequate lighting, and only turning on the central heating when the guests start to turn blue. A slight exaggeration? There are, regrettably, such people who let the trade down, but fortunately they are few. With competition so keen, a reputation for meanness is a label no one can afford.

Most people like being spoiled a little, especially on holiday. Start off the day on the right foot, put yourself out a little; offering fish on the breakfast menu once a week won't break the bank. Even a small point such as this could be the forerunner of healthier bookings in the future.

Useful tips

The subject of food and cooking is so diverse that you may welcome a few tips if you are new to the catering trade.

Arrowroot

This has the edge over cornflour in that it is tasteless and produces a clear thickening for fruit syrups, sauces, some soups and gravies. When used for glazing a fruit flan, arrowroot is ideal as it doesn't obscure the fruit and gives the dish a shiny finish. It makes a nutritive milk pudding for invalids and those with upset stomachs.

Bread

It is unlikely that you will have the time or the energy for making your own bread. Of the many excellent varieties to be bought, just what you stock will depend on the sort of market you cater for; usually, the higher the tariff the greater the variety on offer. However, for an average guest house or hotel, the needs usually run to rolls (mostly white but brown are becoming more popular) for serving with soup and filling for snacks, and pre-cut white or brown bread, the former for toast and to accompany breakfast, and both for sandwiches and toasted snacks. White used to be the norm, but brown bread now appears more often on hotel tables. Even for lunches in modest hotels, the budget can usually run to an assortment when required. French sticks are ideal for ploughman's lunches or for serving with small salads or pâté. Warm both bread and rolls slightly before serving. Slightly stale bread can be made into bread pudding, bread-and-butter pudding, or summer pudding.

Breadcrumbs
Fresh breadcrumbs keep for months in a sealed bag in the freezer. Store dry, fresh white breadcrumbs (dried in the oven without colouring) in an airtight jar. These also keep for months.

Cheese
At dinner, cheese and red wine go together like Derby and Joan. Cheese is such a versatile standby, quite apart from the cheeseboard; it can add interest to a salad, be used au gratin, under the grill or cooked in the oven with all manner of meat, fish and vegetable dishes. Small quantities of Parmesan can be expensive; look for a catering pack for your freezer. Freezing soft cheese is not a good idea.

Chocolate
Children (and many adults) usually love chocolate. It can be grated directly on to ice cream dishes, fruit sundaes and banana splits, made into delicious sauces for serving hot, incorporated into cakes and gateaux and used in a variety of other ways.

Danish pastries
Pre-cooked or home-made with different fillings and toppings, these can be served at tea, lunch, or even as a dessert with single cream.

Dried fruits
No store cupboard is complete without a variety of these. Recipes abound for the use of currants, sultanas, raisins, prunes, apricots and dates.

Fish
Haddock and kippers are both favourites at the breakfast table.

When the top of your cooker is being used to full capacity, try cooking fish in foil parcels in the oven, which also reduces fishy odour. If most of your summer guests are clamouring for fried fish and chips (cod and plaice are excellent) you would do better to leave the stuffed, baked and au gratin fish dishes until later in the year.

Whatever the dish, always buy the freshest and best quality fish available. Most areas have at least one good fresh fish shop. If there are more, try them all. Even if you have to travel further afield, it will be worth it in the long run if the fish itself is worthy; here much will depend on quantities required. Unfortunately, the time factor leads many guest houses and hotels to keep a stock of frozen fish. Prawn cocktail is very popular, served in the height of the summer season when your tariff can embrace the higher cost involved.

Food colourings
Edible and long-lasting, such colourings can be used in a variety of ways (be sparing when in doubt). Marzipan sweets and petit fours would be duller without them, and you can use them to pep up milk drinks and in many imaginative ways.

Frying
Because of the ease with which fat ignites at high temperatures, the greatest care should be taken when frying foods. The use of thermostatically controlled appliances is advisable. *Never* throw water over fat fires; smother them with a blanket, rug or cloth. Ensure that any fats or oils used are of the best quality.

Garnishing
There are countless ways of garnishing or 'decorating' food. Not only can a garnish complement flavours, it can also provide a contrasting texture, add richness to a plain dish, moistness to a dry one, and bring a dish out of the ordinary and into the limelight.

Grapes
Table grapes look attractive alongside (or on) a cheeseboard and are excellent included in a fresh fruit salad. They are also delicious in some poultry and fish dishes.

Herbs
There are so many, but do use them with a light hand. Keep small quantities of dried herbs, which you can replace often. The more common herbs, like mint, thyme, parsley, rosemary and chives are

grown in many a back garden, but how many of us think of growing a bay tree?

Honey
Offer it as an alternative to the breakfast marmalade; it is more popular these days because of the increased interest in health foods.

Lemons
The lemon is an excellent garnish for fish dishes, hot and cold soufflés, ideal in the bar, keeps bananas suitably pale, provides the pectin lacking when making strawberry jam, and makes a refreshing change from milk in tea. Sliced lemon freezes well.

Meat
The quantity of fresh or frozen meat used is purely a personal matter and often one of convenience, but whatever the argument in favour of freezers *nothing* can take the place of, or compare with, fresh food. Along with potatoes, other vegetables and fruit, meat will be a regular purchase (unless you choose to freeze very large quantities). Large joints of meat are more economical than small ones and, even where smaller joints would do, because of the lower shrinkage rate and the convenience of having slices of meat over for sandwiches, to accompany salads, or pop into the freezer, they are a better buy. Remember that joints need a reasonable layer of fat to baste without your help (meat dries up when over-basted). You will need plenty of all the popular meats, such as pork, lamb and beef and, as with fish, concentrate on what your market wants and leave the more sophisticated dishes for weekenders and winter guests.

Menus
À la carte. This is a menu where each dish is individually priced. As dishes are cooked to order, they are naturally more expensive than a set dish which has been pre-cooked.

Table d'hôte. This is French for 'the table of the host' and consists of a set luncheon or dinner menu with a fixed price.

Milk
This versatile and nourishing liquid not only contains all types of nutrients, but is a food in itself. Milk comes dried, homogenised, pasteurised, sterilised, and uht (or long life).

Nuts
These varied 'fruits' can be used in all manner of ways: incorporated in sweet and savoury dishes and chopped, shredded and flaked for topping cakes, puddings etc.

Oranges
This fruit has such an attractive warm glow, and appeals especially to children. It contains vitamin C and can be used in many ways: added to fresh fruit salads and jellies, as a garnish in salads and accompanying some poultry dishes — duck à l'orange springs to mind. It is used in the bar to garnish drinks.

Porridge oats
From time to time, you will doubtless get requests for this warming cereal, so have a small supply available.

Poultry and game
In the busy season, you will probably serve more chicken roast than cooked in any other way (it does seem to be a favourite). But chicken can be prepared in numerous ways, from casseroling to frying, and served with delicious sauces. Duck, too, is quite popular, but not a good idea when catering to a full house on a lower tariff. The famous duck à l'orange can be served when your tariff is adjusted accordingly. Turkey doesn't have to wait for Christmas, and it has the advantage of providing plenty of meat at one time because of its size. Most game birds, pheasant, partridge and grouse, are more at home in establishments where the prices charged can accommodate them nicely.

Rice
Another versatile food. A whole range of sweet and savoury dishes can be made from rice, and it has the advantage of keeping indefinitely. The main types are short grain (or pudding rice), long grain, and brown.

Sauces
Single and double creams are useful, but when there's more time to spare, there are some delicious cream sauces to be made.

Custard. Very popular. Of course, there's custard and custard...

Fruit sauce. Made with ripe, liquidised or puréed fruits, a liqueur can be added for special dishes.

And then there are the hard sauces like brandy, lemon, and rum.

Sausages and salami

The wide assortment of sausages available, from all over Europe, can be a boon for luncheons, as part of an hors-d'oeuvre, or served with salad. For some, breakfast wouldn't be breakfast without the English sausage; children (and grown-ups) enjoy 'bangers and mash', and it keeps good company with poultry.

Sugar

Whether it be brown or white, caster, demerara or lump, there are countless uses for sugar of all kinds, including the sophisticated cousins, vanilla and icing sugar.

Sprinkle sugar over fresh mint; not only is the flavour improved, but the mint is easier to chop. Peas and carrots benefit from a teaspoonful of sugar added during the cooking time. Roast duck or chicken sprinkled with a little sugar will have a crisper skin.

Sweets and puddings

Apple. The cooking apple lends itself so well to many dishes; there's chilled and frothy apple snow, apple sauce for serving with pork and duck, apple pie (mix dried fruit with the apple for a change), baked apple oozing fruit and honey, apple sponge, apple cake and so on: it is also a pleasant surprise in some salads.

Bread-and-butter pudding. An old favourite this — it is still popular and quite delicious served with cream or ice cream. You can use up slightly stale bread to make it.

Flans. Keep several cooked unfilled pastry flan cases on hand, to be used when needed. They can be as elaborate or simple as you have the time for (drained, tinned fruit is good and always in store).

Fruit salad and stewed fruit. Both are welcome after a substantial meal. Some liqueurs and fruit salad blend happily together. Serve the salad with single cream and the stewed fruit with either cream or custard.

Jellies. Not just for the children! Colourful, digestible and the perfect partner for fruit and ice cream. Buy good makes only; some cheaper types have a very synthetic flavour.

Meringue. Whether used for pastries, toppings or as a complete sweet with fruit and liqueur, meringue is popular and can be impressive when cooked with care.

Pancakes. These freeze well so can be made in advance to use when time is short. As a savoury dish, especially for vegetarians, they can be stuffed with an assortment of fillings, topped with cheese and lightly browned. They are superb when filled with chopped or puréed fruit or served flat with sultanas and lemon.

Trifle. A widely popular dessert. Professional cooks would shudder, but there are very passable short-cut catering packets on the market. Traditional, home-made trifles are another story altogether, and can contain all manner of fruit, nuts etc.

Yorkshire pudding. Many look for it when the roast beef makes an entrance. For best results, keep everything (oven and pan) really hot.

Unmoulding
The unmoulding of some desserts can be a bit difficult, so any tips are welcomed. Try smearing a few droplets of water over the serving dish then, if the mould should fall a little to one side, it will be easier to slide and centre it. Just prior to turning out, dip the mould in a large bowlful of hot water for a few moments; using the tips of your fingers, loosen around the edges of the mould. Place the serving dish over the top so that you can invert them together. Give them a quick shake and turn both at the same time. The mould's contents should then be released. Repeat the process if faced with a stubborn jelly or other mould.

Wine
A vast subject. In the kitchen it can be used to enhance many dishes and sauces, and is worth experimenting with. It is an essential ingredient for many gourmet dishes.

Yoghurt
Now very popular. A huge array of plain and fruity ready-mades are available in stores and supermarkets. However, it can be made at home with a commercial yoghurt maker, and eaten with breakfast cereals, fruit, or as an ingredient in some soups, sauces etc.

Drinks

Tea is still the favourite national drink, tea-bags being the most convenient way of buying and serving it, and usually favoured by the catering trade. Delicate or pungent teas are to be found in high-class establishments, where the more discriminating guest will request a particular favourite by name. Although it is more usual for tea to be accompanied by milk, tea served with lemon is most refreshing, particularly after a heavy meal. Serve tea either free after a meal or on request, charging anything from 25p to 30p per cup or 40p to 50p per pot (two cups).

Coffee. Whether you offer instant or ground coffee will depend on taste, preference and the price charged. While instant coffee is chosen by the majority, very many people enjoy ground coffee and the filter method of making it wins on convenience and price. There are many other ways of making coffee but this is a personal choice. Serve it either free after a meal or on request, charging anything from 45p to 50p per cup or 75p to 85p per pot (two cups).

Milk drinks and night-time beverages. Children in particular enjoy milk shakes and there are many flavours from which to choose, both in powdered and liquid form. Milk-shake mixers are handy machines for making them. Ovaltine, Horlicks, drinking chocolate and Bournvita are popular with those not propping up your bar. Serve on request, charging from 35p to 45p each for bedtime drinks and milk shakes (the latter would be served in a glass).

Fruit juices etc. While tomato juice is occasionally asked for, it is not a particularly popular drink. Favourites seem to be orange, apple and pineapple. They can be purchased in large bottles or cartons for the dining-room, and in small cans for the bar. Most children seem to prefer fizzy drinks like coke or lemonade.

Wine. White wine is particularly popular for serving with meals, but demands for dry, medium or sweet fluctuate. It should be served chilled. Red wine is served at room temperature or even slightly warmer. Opened bottles should not be kept more than a day or so, and you may wish to consider buying boxed wine for serving by the glass.

Spirits and liqueurs are long lasting; stock the basics and possibly a modest supply only of anything currently being promoted on television.

Beer is mentioned in the bar section on page 82. Always have a reasonable selection of cans and bottles; serve cool or at room temperature, and watch the 'use by' dates on the containers.

Sherry. Dry sherry or fino should be used within a day or so of being opened; medium and sweet sherries (amontillado and oloroso) last longer and are more popular.

Chapter 11
Charging

The great variation in hotel charges is dictated by venue, density of hotels, volume of business and the specific type and standards of the hotel.

Up-market hotels

It is generally accepted that, where a hotel is situated in an enviable position, is decorated and turned out to a high standard, offers an excellent menu, *and* has attractive grounds, gardens, bar or other feature, the tariff will be considerably higher than those of hotels where the standards are more basic. Higher tariffs are usually justifiable, for the upkeep of such places is much greater than many members of the public appreciate. There are extra staff to consider, more expensive food, and more amenities. It can add up to a pretty penny.

Where adjoining or nearby hotels are of a similar high standard, and size, it is found that tariffs compare favourably from the public's point of view and, even where one hotel is that much smaller, here again, general appearance, decor and menu can attract the discriminating guest.

If there is a high density of hotels, different types and sizes are usually grouped in separate areas; it is unusual to find a modest guest house sandwiched between two very grand neighbours, although it may happen from time to time. Where the larger hotels are concerned, the charges for offering a sumptuous suite with private bathroom and balcony, first-class room service and an indoor heated swimming pool, naturally, will be on the hefty side!

The modest guest house or hotel seems like the poor relation in comparison with the above, but it has much to offer to many people.

Smaller hotels of similar type

Where a modest hotel is situated in an area surrounded by, say, 20 similar-sized and types of hotels and guest houses, there is usually little difference in the tariffs charged, even if one or two of the establishments in the area or stretch of road leave something to be desired. This is sometimes frustrating for those who warrant the top of the tariff prices. Charge too high a tariff in such circumstances to counteract the problem, and it is doubtful if you would attract the same volume of business, particularly passing trade, as your neighbour (even though the hedge is trim and the hotel inviting). When geared to cater for certain sections of the public, tariffs cannot be too out of step with similar premises; people with lower incomes do shop around looking for value for money. I have often been aware of situations where very pleasing hotels, charging say £2 per night more, are sited among less attractive — though fair hotels — and the former have been only half full. To balance this, the same type of hotel in an up-market setting is more likely to have visitors flocking around its doors. The fact that *your* breakfast may be a most pleasant surprise compared with maybe a quarter of the other hotels in the road, is not known to those first-timers perusing your tariff in the hall.

Low hotel-density areas

A very different situation exists when hotels are thinner on the ground. If you are fortunate enough to purchase a hotel, say, on the outskirts of an historic town or in a venue with some strong tourist attraction tariff-fixing (again depending on the proximity of other hotels) can be much more fluid. There is bound to be a rash of 'classy' hotels around such places but, even if you are running a 'middle-of-the-road' business, you are in a more favourable position, tariff-wise, than proprietors running similar businesses in more densely hotel-populated areas. It is generally considered that competition is healthy, and it is; however, very little competition can, sometimes, be even healthier! Where there is a scarcity of accommodation, you could even find yourself with the monopoly if situated in a really good spot and competing favourably in all respects — particularly if you have something special to offer the public.

Sadly, there are a few hoteliers who, finding themselves in such a position and independent of the market constraints that operate elsewhere, get greedy and give the trade a bad name. But most hoteliers in favourable situations work extremely hard, do not over-exploit their position, and go on to higher, and much deserved, financial rewards.

One very important point to bear in mind is that smaller towns and large villages are 'fair weather' spots when compared with larger towns and seaside resorts, which usually have more to offer in the way of distraction when the weather is unfavourable. This must be taken into account when assessing what your *yearly* takings are likely to be, and this is where the higher tariff comes into play.

High hotel-density areas

If you are buying a hotel in a high-density seaside resort, the examples given below may be helpful when deciding what the following year's charges are going to be although, of course, these are purely hypothetical. You will need to prune or raise your own tariff in keeping with personal circumstances and the business around you. But, first, a little homework is necessary:

1. Enquire of the vendor what his charges have been during the past year, and what tariff he would recommend for the following year. (This is only a rough guide for he may suggest a higher tariff than is practicable to enhance business prospects.)
2. Even if satisfied with the vendor's suggested tariff, discuss it with your accountant; he may have one or two valuable points to make.
3. Investigate the immediate area where you intend to operate and note tariffs charged, types of guest houses and hotels, and the general appearance of all the property inspected.

Taking all this into consideration, you can then come to your own conclusion (bearing your outgoings in mind) whether your hotel should stay *exactly* in line with neighbouring businesses, ie, charge, say, £14 per night for bed and breakfast and £21 for bed, breakfast and evening meal. Or, where your guest house or hotel is perhaps slightly smaller, has fewer facilities, or is generally more modest, reduce these charges by a pound. (For the sake of simplicity, VAT is ignored.)

If, on the other hand, your property is detached, with larger than average garden or grounds and an interesting or particularly inviting frontage, you could raise your tariff by £1 to £2, perhaps more, per person. And, where your facilities are better than most in the area (perhaps there are showers en suite in several of the bedrooms) an extra charge may be made for this. Shower-room charges range from around £7 to £10 per week (not per person); although it is liable to fluctuate depending on area and hotel, an average charge in a modest hotel is usually about £8. However, as rooms with showers en suite are becoming more evident, an inclusive charge is often made.

Whatever charges you decide upon to cover the bulk of the summer season, and this, naturally, will have to be planned beforehand because of the printing of tariff cards and brochures, variation of such a tariff, where necessary, is purely a personal matter and often one of common sense.

In practice, whatever limitations are seemingly imposed by the price-structuring of hotels and guest houses around you, and in face of the existing tariff charged or suggested by your predecessor for the coming season, tariffs have to be modified by reason of differing overheads and outgoings. The theory and practice of the situation rarely tally, particularly in a high hotel-density area. This should not necessarily indicate that you rush off and buy a hotel in a quiet area, where the season is often shorter!

Take a situation where — in June — the weather is poor, hoteliers are playing a game of spot the visitor, and a lady arrives on your doorstep enquiring about your tariff. The fact that it was fixed at, say, £80 per week inclusive for bed, breakfast and evening meal shouldn't stop you — if she hesitates — from offering such a holiday for £75. If she accepts the £75 price, returns *and* recommends you, the 'lost' £5 will not be lost at all. With hotels all around only a quarter filled (including yours) you would be unwise not to make such an offer.

Conversely, in a situation where the summer sun is beating down relentlessly (and the visitors are beating on your door) you can politely refuse a couple (where you have a room vacant with a double and single bed available) and wait until a couple with a child or teenager comes along. They often do!

Your costs

Take a couple who have bought their hotel outright, have no bank loan to worry about, and have been in business for, say, three years; they are obviously better placed to reduce their tariff should they wish to, or abide by that imposed by neighbours and, provided they run their business sensibly, could go from strength to strength. It is much more of a struggle for the couple who owe around £55,000 or more, start off 'cold' as far as reputation is concerned and have several expensive purchases to make. In their case, progress can be slow and arduous, but everyone has to start somewhere! It is, naturally, the main aim to make as high a profit as you can or, at the very least, break even. Unfortunately, the reality of the situation is that it is difficult to make an actual profit in the first few years of trading unless one is well-heeled to start with, or extremely lucky. If profit alone is what you require, then before you start up, consider the return your savings would produce from investment and compare it with what you could expect from hotel keeping.

The hotel trade differs from others in that one's charges tend to be dictated by the local competition, and it is up to the hotelier to provide the best service he can and still make a profit, whereas in most trades, an article or service is costed, overheads and profit margin added on, and the customer pays the final figure, or something near it.

Quite apart from any sums you have worked out for yourself, observations made and advice given by the vendor, your best course of action would be to have a meeting with your accountant. He will be familiar with general outgoings and overheads and will know, after talking to you, what your specific outgoings and overheads are likely to be. You can then draw up a suitable tariff between you, assessed by:

1. Your bank loan and interest charges, fixed overheads and flexible outgoings, *and*
2. Taking into account what competitors charge. However reluctantly, concessions have to be made at times to keep your business competitive and a lure to the public.

Generally speaking, outgoings are higher in the first year of trading. Not only are there one or more items of furniture to replace, or carpets to be renewed, there may be a need to modernise a kitchen or completely redecorate one or two rooms. And where facilities are basic, you may feel there is a need to introduce one or more showers en suite. Having taken care of any glaring faults plus the above during your first year, and taking into account that proprietors automatically raise their tariffs by between 5 and 10 per cent in most years, it can be seen that, providing business is as brisk, there is a higher chance of breaking even or making a small profit in the second year of trading.

There should be no reason why a slightly higher profit could not be made in your third year of trading because of the decreasing need for replacements, etc. As time passes, of course, expenditure will fluctuate as the need arises for expenditure on paintwork, wallpaper, bedding, and replacements generally which, in turn, should be balanced by better trade because of a, hopefully, growing reputation.

Flexibility of tariff

Your tariff is bound to vary over the period of a whole year because of seasonal demand. From late December through until Easter, it should be prudently lower (as in late October through until Christmas), but flexibility is the keynote when planning your charges, particularly in respect of embracing bank holidays and the Christmas break. Take the Easter holiday as an example: whether a charge is made on a daily or an 'all-in' three-day period basis, it should be a little higher than the preceding week or the period immediately following. The same principle should apply to other bank holidays. Just how much your tariff fluctuates is dependent on the density of hotels and popularity of the area, heavier outgoings, weather etc (for previously fixed tariffs can be changed at the drop of a hat if necessary). Naturally, at Christmas, the tariff would be appreciably higher to cover extra food and drink, plus all the festive trimmings, decorations, cost of pantomime and any outings.

Special and gourmet weekends are another consideration, and tariffs have to be in step and as flexible as service and menu decree. It seems superfluous to state that any additional outgoings have to be taken into account to prevent running at a loss.

Letting of double rooms at single rates

Policies vary from one hotel to another; much depends on the time of year and how full the hotel is. It would obviously be unbusiness-like where there was one double room vacant, to let such a room to a single gentleman. Even if an extra charge was made, it wouldn't bring in the same income as when let to two people (although some hoteliers do let double rooms to single people in the busy season provided they pay the double rate). However, one person wouldn't spend the same amount of money on extras or in the bar as two. Nevertheless, it would be equally unbusiness-like not to let a single person have a double room — where your single rooms are full — at a *single* (or fractionally higher) rate during a quiet period.

Rates for children

Charges for children vary up and down the country, again depending on the time of year, and the attitude of the proprietors of specific establishments. As a more obvious example, take a family hotel. For a family room accommodating mum, dad and, say, two children, one aged two and one aged six, in the height of the season, the elder child would most likely either be booked in at half or three quarters of the adult rate, and a charge for the younger child waived. Or in some cases, the elder would be charged half and a nominal charge of around £18 to £20 made for the infant. Some larger hotels may charge higher rates for both children, depending on their ages, which is to be expected.

A full charge should be (and normally is) made where a child is over 13 — some can eat you out of house and home. Again, flexibility is required where a double booking involving four adults and five children is concerned and the prices charged are pointedly queried. Pruning is prudent (especially when business is slow).

Where babies (up to a year or 18 months) are concerned, it is optional whether a charge is made or not. A nominal sum of about £18 per week is fair where the sterilising of bottles, provision of milk and small meals are involved. Again, it depends on the size of the family, how much you like children (and more specifically babies!) and how much goodwill you wish to promote. Even some family hotels discourage babies for all the obvious reasons.

Other reasons for high or low tariff-fixing
If the same family has run a hotel for many years and owns the property, such established people are in the enviable position of being free to vary their tariff more than newcomers, for obvious reasons. Higher tariffs are essential in very seasonal areas, especially where the weather is fickle.

Pets are dealt with on page 76.

Chapter 12

Getting Known

If you take over an existing hotel, it should already be in the telephone directory and the Yellow Pages; if you are starting up, then make sure you have suitable entries under the right business heading (Guest Houses, Hotels and Inns — even in both) in your local Yellow Pages and any other business directories. Make yourself known at your nearest tourist office or the town hall information office, and see that they have copies of your printed tariff or prospectus.

Passing trade will be your cheapest source of income — you will have already invested in your shop-window (do see that the appearance of your hotel speaks for itself). Next comes word-of-mouth — the most gratifying — and after that, luck combined with shrewd advertising.

Advertising media

Do your homework thoroughly. Get to know which advertising medium fulfils your need, not the other way around. If gullible, you can fall victim to all sorts of advertising ploys. Telephone advertising is as common as the postal variety (and the more irritating and time-consuming when the campaigns start). Telephone salespeople, adept at their job, can be very convincing and persuasive. Good money can all too easily follow good money, and bad timing can mean money down the drain. Budget well and plan carefully; impetuous spending can cost you dear.

Holiday magazines are well worth exploring as a suitable medium for your advertising — some appear monthly, others quarterly or yearly; the annual local holiday guide in particular gives value for money, also *Weekender* and REPTA, the railway members' holiday guide. The Civil Service has its own publication, the *CPSA Holiday Guide*. Do check on circulation figures and areas covered. One-off advertisements can be such a gamble. Despite its jungle of offers, *Dalton's Weekly* has an excellent, country-wide circulation and seems to appeal to a large cross-section of the public. In common with many papers, it offers proportionate reductions on the number of advertisements running concurrently. Careful advertising should pay off — and continue to do so —provided you keep your end of the bargain. Just two guests returning twice and ultimately recommending you more than justifies the initial outlay. Your local tourist board can offer useful advice.

Quite apart from the usual ads, consider having posters printed (perhaps sharing business and costs with a neighbouring hotel). These can then be circulated to clubs, displayed in shop windows or on notice-boards in various locations. Posters at the railway, coach and bus stations are seen by all but car travellers.

After some trial and error (it wouldn't be human to make no mistakes) you will get to know which media are right for you. Of course, depending on what you are offering and the season, the wording of your advertisements is bound to vary. You may wish to diversify — two different advertisements in two papers — one a simple but attractive lure for the general public, and one to attract a 'specialist market'. Perhaps you enjoy cooking vegetarian dishes? Highlight and cash in on any special facility to hand. If you are close to a golf course, bowling green or tennis court, spell it out. That you are adjacent to, or a couple of hundred yards from, say, a golf course, is your ace card. Don't keep it up your sleeve. Where relevant, make enquiries as to names and addresses of golf, tennis or bowling clubs throughout the country and write to as many as possible offering your services. It will be well worth while.

When planning to cater for the more discerning palate, or specialising in vegetarian or health foods, for example, a mention in *The Lady* wouldn't come amiss, particularly if you are situated away from the more popular built-up seaside resorts. A browse through the specialist magazines in the larger bookstores would be useful too. Also, should you wish to attract customers from specific countries or ethnic areas, an advertisement placed in one of the many appropriate local papers should do the trick.

Advertisement content

Make sure that your advertisement copy is clear and easy to read and understand. Have you given your address and telephone number, so the customer can respond quickly? If you include a photograph, will it be clear in the final ad, or be reduced to a grey smudge? Use a good drawing rather than an unsatisfactory photo.

Place emphasis on good food, comfort and (in the quieter seasons) a 'restful atmosphere' and, if your property is situated in a flattish area, say so. 'No hills' is icing on the cake for a large proportion of the older community. Conversely, if situated in hillier regions, outline details of transport available and emphasise the beautiful views. You may find it worthwhile to offer a personal pick-up service: 'Personal pick-up service — from coach or train. We are only a phone call away', surely a lure for someone with carbuncles or arthritis.

Broadly speaking, whatever market you appeal to, it isn't a secret that people of all ages seek good food, cooked with care, comfort, cleanliness, friendliness, some entertainment and accessible facilities. It is up to you to put across to the sea of expectant faces out there — as potently as you can — just what your hotel in particular has to offer. If the wording and presentation of your advertisement are crudely and impetuously contrived, and say nothing special to sing your praises, the reaction will be negative. Very likely, the searching digit will move on! Do offer the public a tempting package; offer to spoil them. And, for those who succumb to temptation, carry out your promise, and more seeds of future business are sown.

If at all possible, before the purchase, stay at the hotel of your choice for a weekend or longer, for it is vital to the progress of your business to gauge your predecessor's reputation. Remember, part of the purchase price is termed goodwill. See, first-hand, what you have to live up to, or overcome. You can then word your 'début' advertisement accordingly. Following in the aromatic wake of a chef of renown, emphasise that your standards will be as high. If, on the other hand, you have a bad reputation to overcome, stress 'new caring owners' and that the cuisine will be 'par excellence'.

Special offers or events

If you are large enough, you can offer special reductions for parties (coach companies will welcome you and, in turn, will give you reasonable and special rates) or if small, consider sharing a coach party with your neighbouring hotel (provided their standards are as good as yours). Also contact as many holiday agents as you can; there are dozens to choose from. If your proposals are attractive enough, a representative may be sent along to look your hotel over. A few block bookings are a comfort when things seem a bit slow.

A point to remember is that you don't have to put all your eggs in one basket. While trying to appeal to one section of the community, there is nothing to stop you offering 'gourmet weekends' at bargain prices out of the summer season. If your talents lie in that direction, such weekends would offer you variety and scope, and be a challenge too. Likewise, should you employ a chef, he would doubtless welcome the opportunity of displaying his epicurean skills. There are numerous themes which can be followed for such weekends.

If *during the summer* you decided to extend a welcome to, say, senior citizens in particular in the autumn and winter seasons, special reference to the reduced tariff must be made in your advertisements. Value for money is what the public is after — not everyone has a nest egg. Be as competitive in price as you can possibly afford for, surely, it is better to have at least half your rooms filled at a reduced tariff than two at the usual rate. Special offers like 'four persons for the price of three' or 'for the third person sharing a large room with two others, accommodation free of charge!' won't go unnoticed. It is not uncommon for parties of ladies to holiday together.

Sources of business

From time to time, banks, large organisations, airports etc, entertain overseas visitors, along with members of the public and the world of commerce. You have nothing to lose — and much to gain — by writing to some of them, offering your services, especially for business lunches or dinners. You could offer a large room to them for meetings.

During the winter it is worth considering taking in students from local colleges. When their term starts in September each year, many have difficulty in finding permanent accommodation and others need somewhere on a short-term basis. Many hoteliers take in students from September until the following Easter, or later. It is a personal choice. If you are interested, do contact colleges early in the summer, as lists of likely accommodation are kept and referred to before the summer holidays start in July. If you have bedrooms large enough to house two or three students comfortably — bearing in mind they need desks or tables, good reading lights, and so on — the reduced tariff you are obliged to adhere to (individual colleges will advise you here) is justified by the sharing. Should your hotel be chosen for students, an official from the college will need to inspect the room to be let, and possibly your dining-room, kitchen and residents' lounge. Students can help the business to tick over when other guests are few, and provide welcome bread-and-butter money.

Chapter 13
Staying Ahead of the Competition

You will always need to think of the future, and of keeping your hotel full as much of the time as possible. The immediately available way is to make guests so welcome that they return and bring their friends. Here are some tips on ways to do this.

Encourage your guests to return

Greet your guests by offering them a welcome cup of tea or coffee on the house; a surprising number of small hotels do not, more's the shame. Apart from refreshing a visitor after a long journey, it does help to make the first-time guest feel at home.

Point out the location of toilets and bathrooms to guests immediately upon their arrival. This may sound obvious, but some older people become slightly agitated if unclear as to where such facilities are situated. American visitors invariably ask to inspect the bathroom(s) before their bedroom.

Establish immediately upon arrival whether your guests have any positive food fads; one guest I recall had a phobia about chicken and couldn't stand the sight of one let alone the taste! Another was allergic to butter, another to anything really cold. It's the knowing that counts.

Arrival day can be a strained experience for both guest and hotelier but remember you are in the pilot's seat. Some weeks the hotelier's lot is made easier by the arrival of parties, be they family or friends. The atmosphere is at once less tense than when all of your guests are, more or less, strangers to each other. When this happens and there is a 'comedian' or 'character' in their midst, you will bless him. The others will soon be uncoiling their locks. Come Monday, once you know individual likes and dislikes plus details of a few hysterectomies and how someone's Uncle Arthur practically won the Second World War single-handed, it will all come together and, from then on, should be plain sailing until departure day.

Rules and regulations scribbled on scraps of card or paper and pinned willy nilly are untidy and mostly unnecessary. A small and neat (professionally printed) reminder in loos and bathrooms about necessary hygiene is sufficient. If you do insist on lots of rules and regulations (too many will put people off) ensure that they are properly printed and neatly displayed. Printed fire precaution leaflets are provided by the Fire Department; these should be firmly placed on the inside of each bedroom door, where they can be plainly seen. Cards with a greeting to the guest, times of meals, etc can be either pinned over the mantelpiece in the bedroom or placed on it for easy reading. However, even when such cards are in evidence, personal communication is still appreciated. Even the briefest (hopefully pleasant) encounter between guest and host or hostess paves the way for a relaxed holiday. Once a guest feels at home, half the battle is won!

Be prepared to offer children an alternative to the set meal (many youngsters dislike vegetables and plain or creamed potatoes); it is not difficult to provide hamburgers, fish fingers or chicken drumsticks and French fries — their main favourites. When it comes to desserts, just let your fancy take flight and, if you hide a few small sweets (like smarties or chocolate buttons) in ice cream dishes occasionally, it will keep the little darlings quiet for a while! Colour and presentation count for a lot when catering for children.

Always provide jugs of fresh water for each table.

Do check that the salt flows freely (a few grains of rice help), and that sauce-bottle tops are not a congealed mess. Marmalade reacts quickly when placed in direct sunlight and forms a white froth in next to no time, so avoid this.

Where husbands/wives/friends mention it in advance, see that birthdays and anniversaries are a little special. Bake or buy a suitable cake; add a more glamorous table-setting — be it flowers, napkins, decorated napkin rings, candles or wine; place a small greetings card on the table; play a favourite tune if you have the record or tape — or 'Happy Birthday', 'Anniversary Waltz', etc.

No need to panic or refuse a booking at the mention of 'vegetarian' or 'health' food. There are countless easy-to-make dishes; just take a deep breath and dive into your cookery books. The same remarks apply when catering for diabetics or people with specific dietary problems. It is rare to have a combination all in one week.

Even when making nominal charges, there is quite a good profit margin on sandwiches; see that yours are extra fresh, imaginative and tasty. Regular orders for packed lunches are to be welcomed, as are late snacks and hot drinks.

Ensure that a comprehensive supply of brochures, pamphlets and posters is displayed in your reception area, advertising what the resort or locality has to offer the holiday-maker. Offer directions in the form of a map to available entertainments.

Make the most of special holidays, like Easter and Christmas. At Easter, give any children staying (if not everyone) a small Easter egg at breakfast. Decorate your sideboard or serving tables with chicks, baskets of eggs etc. Make or buy simnel cake.

Christmas is very hard work and a demanding time for all hotel proprietors, but it can be rewarding and great fun if one enters into the festive spirit of the occasion.

One advantage when catering at Christmas is that November and the early part of December are, more often than not, quieter times than usual, enabling proprietors and chefs to prepare for the holiday in a more leisurely fashion than is the norm in summer. The cooking of Christmas cakes and puddings can be a less hurried procedure, and freezers can be checked and restocked by buying well in advance of the Christmas break (when prices are lower). Three- or four-day bookings are the more common, and mostly consist of full board, with festive extras included.

It is usual for guests to be greeted with a sherry/wine/champagne welcome. A Christmas tree is usually the focal point, bedecked in traditional splendour, and a small gift for each guest is either tied to the tree or placed at their table setting. Decorations can be as restrained or ostentatious as individual taste — and energy — runs. Most hotels include at least some of the drinks in the price (usually the wine with dinner). Again, much depends on the proprietor's generosity and on the tariff charged. Try to organise a Fancy Dress parade and at least some party games and, of course, provide plenty of music. Many all-in breaks offer a pantomime as part of the 'deal' (a nice break for you too) and/or a coach trip into the surrounding countryside. There are all sorts of ways to entertain your guests — it is up to you to see that they have a Christmas to remember. (We put sparklers in the Christmas puddings one year and doused the lights; it was simple but effective.) Some guests will boycott all your plans and opt for snoozing in front of the box. Let them! It's their choice and their holiday. Just how well everything goes does depend a lot on the crowd you have; one Christmas crowd is never like the next! You can pull out all the stops with Christmas fare, and the more imaginative, colourful and tasty your table, the more bookings you are likely to have for the following year.

If a festive Christmas is not to your taste, you can offer a 'Christmas in retreat' for like-minded guests.

Competition from larger hotels

When considering the competition from the larger hotels, it has to be accepted that you fill a different need. However, it doesn't always follow that the 'well-heeled' will steer clear of your hotel just because it is modest in size and situated among other, modest businesses. (One early spring day, a lady who was very comfortably off indeed booked into our modest hotel; she was recovering from a traumatic divorce and simply wanted the peace and quiet we could afford her. As guests were few and far between, we were more than able to cater for her needs.) And there are many people, well able to meet the higher tariffs charged in larger hotels, who enjoy the personal service and homely touches that are virtually impossible in such places. Bearing this in mind, it is certainly worth ensuring that your property is attractive both inside and out, that the food you serve is the best your budget can safely accommodate, and that every attention is given to those small touches in surroundings and service.

Competing on an entertainment basis with larger hotels is more or less impossible. Tariffs of such hotels can easily take in the provision of a dance floor and band or group, or perhaps a resident pianist and, occasionally, cabaret acts. However, there is still much that can be done on a different level. Most caring hotels provide music, either with meals, or during the evenings, although it is important that such music should not be so loud as to drown conversation or jar people's nerves, and it is also only fair to give thought to the selection of records or tapes you offer. Try to build up a stock, and see that it includes everything from Tosca to Tommy Steele, Puccini to 'Police'. When business is quiet and there are half a dozen youngsters or senior citizens in the hotel, they think much of being catered for in such a way. However, the use of taped music will involve the payment of an annual fee to the Performing Rights Society. A small hotel or guest house with up to 15 rooms should allow £28.36 plus £14.18 in the first year and £28.36 thereafter (this may be subject to a review).

A colour television set is, of course, a must; two if possible and, if you have a games room or snooker/pool table or whatever, it is a definite attraction. I do know of one or two 'guitar-strumming proprietors', and of a couple of amateur organists, so there must be more around. And I am aware of one or two hotels where there is a minute dance floor. If you neither strum, play the organ nor have a dance floor, put your thinking cap on.

Whatever steps you take to improve your hotel to compete for trade, and however fetching the end result, in the long run, value for money is what the public in general is after.

Once you know that the hotel opposite — while looking marvellous — has a gloomy interior and gloomier proprietors, and that the cook in the hotel next door would be better employed driving a train or assembling cars, you can concentrate on investigating what others nearby have to offer. Of course, those few hotels with peeling facades stand little chance with passing trade when business is slow and the weather bad.

Whatever the competition, a pleasing appearance and general desirability overall go a long way, and are *so* important in luring passing trade in particular. It is up to you, when situated cheek by jowl with hotels presenting a well-manicured garden and a beautiful 'face' for all and sundry to admire, to do everything in your power to compare favourably. Sometimes, there is a simple solution — perhaps an 'all-over' treatment with dazzling white paint, the planting of unusual or attractive plants, bushes or small trees either side of the path leading to your hotel, or flanking the entrance-way itself or, a little more ambitious, a new entrance porch, offset by luxurious hanging baskets. Maybe you should rethink your hotel signs. Are they prominent enough? Eyecatching in design and colour treatment? Does your hotel loom dark and ominous as dusk descends? While you don't have to emulate the Blackpool illuminations (some do) subtle lighting can only add to the required welcoming effect.

Once you have cornered the passing trade you can set about dealing with other aspects of competition and see if you can come up with something more original than your neighbours.

Hotels with bars

Although the bar is dealt with in Chapter 7, an appealing and well-stocked bar does count for a lot. Some advertisements place much emphasis on: 'Our Tudor bar — come along and enjoy a drink with your friends', or lure the public: 'Come to our Bat-Cave bar if you dare...' There is no doubt that hotels with outstandingly eyecatching and well-stocked bars have the edge for some members of the public, and it doesn't always follow that such bars are housed in the larger hotels. If you are hemmed in by hotels offering such facilities, waste no time and either apply for a licence (if you are without one) or give your bar the benefit of a critical eye, and perhaps a new look.

Competing with food or entertainment

Having passed the exterior and bar 'barriers', we move on to food. It cannot be emphasised enough that, having 'captured' your guests with the cunning cosmetic job out front, and the promise of lubrication of their vocal chords inside, the trump card is, undoubtedly, your table.

Apart from speaking glowingly of their other assets, hoteliers' advertisements sometimes linger on cuisine, you will observe, and rightly so; there's nothing like spelling it out where a large advertisement is concerned. If particularly proud of your English breakfast (remember for only 50p per person more on the tariff, you could offer kidneys and include fish dishes more often) say so. You may have an extra-special way of cooking a traditional dish. Set out your menu in black and white, giving much thought to the wording. You may not be able to compete with 'Edwardian' or 'Victorian' evenings — which are perhaps best left to up-market hotels — and, anyway, your guests would probably be happier with more simple, down-to-earth dishes — but you can provide a more varied choice of plain, good food and underline that it is 'home-cooked with care'. The few guest houses/hotels who over-indulge themselves in the use of obviously pre-cooked, *cheaper* meals, and serve an overdose of tinned, frozen and synthetic food items soon gain a bad reputation with the more discerning guest. This does not mean, however, that you should ignore many of the excellent products on the market which aid the busy cook, just that, wherever practicable and possible, you should concentrate on fresh ingredients and home-cooked dishes. Take the popular meal of fish and chips; the hotels either side of you may cook a mean piece of fish and a praiseworthy chip, but serve it plain, with perhaps just the addition of a portion of peas. It is surprising the difference a twist of lemon, a lettuce leaf and a sprig of watercress can make for eye-appeal! Anyone who has taken a catering course will garnish any meal as a matter of fact and such touches are commonplace in larger and more up-market hotels, but some of the smaller hotels do forget such trimmings occasionally, which is a shame. And, although you should cater for your particular market, there is nothing to stop originality from creeping into presentation. Hors-d'oeuvres, main courses and desserts will all benefit, as should your business.

Study the contents of advertisements

It is certainly not a futile task to scour the advertising papers, holiday magazines and booklets on the market; just an hour or two reading the contents of such material can reveal much. It is a help to know what you are up against. Once you have 'isolated' your holiday area in such reading matter, study individual advertisements for wording used, facilities offered and any gimmicky aspect there may be. Ideas often feed off themselves; just one good idea — or maybe an old one in a new overcoat — can either revitalise your own advertising or provide the means to pep up trade. Even quite whiskered themes can create interest, drum up business and, despite the necessary planning and work entailed, provide a little light relief for the organisers. More elaborate plans should, of course, be left until the autumn or spring when you will have more time and energy, and when you can stretch the tariff somewhat.

Low-priced competition

Registered hotels and guest houses are often at a disadvantage from private householders who open their doors to holiday business, charging a much lower tariff than professional establishments. Their overheads are comparatively low and they often have several members of the family at work. They rarely advertise, so pick up passing trade by putting a notice in the window.

Summing up

You need to be aware of:

1. *Larger hotels*
   There is really no contest here; some people will always prefer a larger hotel, with grander public rooms and amenities, even if the service offered is poor.

2. *External appearances*
   The competition here is between smaller hotels to lure the passing trade. The better the image, the more passing trade is likely to be attracted.

3. *Food and entertainment*
   Know your limitations as to menu (to fit market and budget requirements) but do your utmost within those limitations to compete with those around you.
   Entertainment is a trickier problem, but it can be overcome without too much expense.

4. *'Pirate' guest houses*
   These places shouldn't have more than a minimal effect on your business.

5. *Subtle, clever, even gimmicky advertising*
   Brisk business can be the direct result of timely and well-thought out advertising, so the ball is in your court.

Appendix

Further reading

An ABC of the Licensing Law, National Union of Licensed Victuallers, Boardman House, 2 Downing Street, Farnham, Surrey

Choosing and Using Professional Advisers, Paul Chaplin (Kogan Page)

Croner's Reference Book for the Self-employed and Smaller Business (Croner Publications)

Food and Beverage Service, D R Lillicrap (Edward Arnold)

Guardian Guide to Running a Small Business, The, 7th edn, ed Clive Woodcock (Kogan Page)

How to Buy a Business, 2nd edn, Peter Farrell (Kogan Page)

How to Double Your Profits Within the Year, John Fenton (Pan Books)

How to Manage Money, C D Dunleavy and M Metcalfe (The Sunday Telegraph)

Law for the Small Business, The Daily Telegraph Guide, 6th edn, Patricia Clayton (Kogan Page)

Questions on Theory of Catering, Kinton and Ceserani (Edward Arnold)

Raising Finance: the Guardian Guide for the Small Business, 3rd edn, Clive Woodcock (Kogan Page)

Running Your Own Bed and Breakfast, Elizabeth Gundrey (Piatkus)

Running Your Own Catering Business, Ursula Garner and Judy Ridgway (Kogan Page)

Understand Your Accounts, 2nd edn, A St J Price (Kogan Page)

Working for Yourself: the Daily Telegraph Guide to Self-employment, 11th edn, Godfrey Golzen (Kogan Page)

Journals

Catering, 30 Calderwood Street, London SE18 6QH

Hotel and Catering Today, 38 Westgate Street,
  Ipswich IP1 3ED

Caterer and Hotelkeeper, Quadrant House, The Quadrant,
  Sutton, Surrey SM2 5AS

The Publican, Maclaren House, 19 Scarbrook Road, Croydon,
  Surrey CR9 1QH

Useful addresses

National telephone dialling codes are given, though local codes
may differ.

Local councils, tourist boards and Chambers of Commerce can
be good sources of help and information. Many organisations
listed below will have local offices.

Advisory, Conciliation and Arbitration Service (ACAS)
  Head Office, 27 Wilton Street, London SW1X 7AZ;
  01-210 3600

Alliance of Small Firms and Self-Employed People
  33 The Green, Calne, Wiltshire SN11 8DJ; 0249 817003

British Hotels, Restaurants and Caterers Association
  40 Duke Street, London W1M 6HR; 01-499 6641

British Insurance Brokers Association
  BIBA House, 14 Bevis Marks, London EC3A 7NT;
  01-623 9043

Department of Employment Small Firms Service
  Freefone Enterprise for all regional offices.

Food and Drink Industries Council
  25 Victoria Street, London SW1H 0EX; 01-222 1533

Health and Safety Executive
  Baynard's House, 1-13 Chepstow Place, Westbourne Grove,
  London W2 4TS; 01-229 3456

HM Customs and Excise
  VAT Administration Directorate, King's Beam House,
  Mark Lane, London EC3R 7HE; 01-626 1515

Hotel Catering and Institutional Management Association
  191 Trinity Road, London SW17 7HN; 01-672 4251

Institute of Chartered Accountants in England and Wales
  PO Box 433, Chartered Accountants' Hall, Moorgate Place,
  London EC2P 2BJ; 01-628 7060

Maltsters' Association of Great Britain
  31B Castlegate, Newark-on-Trent, Nottinghamshire
  NG24 1AZ; 0636 700781

Performing Rights Society Ltd
  29 Berners Street, London W1A 4PP; 01-580 5544

Phonographic Performance Ltd
  Ganton House, 14 Ganton Street, London W1B 1LB;
  01-437 0311

Registrar of Companies
  Companies House, Crown Way, Maindy, Cardiff CF4 3UZ;
  0222 388588

  102 George Street, Edinburgh EH2 3DJ; 031-225 5774

  43-7 Chichester Street, Belfast BT1 4RJ; 0232 234121

Rural Development Commission (replaces CoSIRA)
  141 Castle Street, Salisbury, Wiltshire SP1 3TP;
  0722 336255

Wine and Spirit Education Trust Ltd
  Five Kings House, Kennet Wharf Lane, Upper Thames Street,
  London EC4V 3AJ; 01-236 3551

The Wine Standards Board
  Wine Inspectorate, 68½ Upper Thames Street,
  London EC4V 3BJ; 01-236 9512

Index